Taxation and the Distribution of Income

This is a volume in the series Research Studies of the Fair Tax Commission of Ontario. The Fair Tax Commission's research publication series is intended to inform public discussion of tax policy issues. In making this report available, the commission does not necessarily endorse the results or recommendations of the authors.

Taxation and the Distribution of Income

SHEILA BLOCK and RICHARD SHILLINGTON

KEN BATTLE and SHERRI TORJMAN

BRIAN MURPHY, ROSS FINNIE,

and MICHAEL WOLFSON

edited by

ALLAN M. MASLOVE

Published by University of Toronto Press in cooperation with
the Fair Tax Commission of Ontario

UNIVERSITY OF TORONTO PRESS
Toronto Buffalo London

Printed in Canada
Reprinted in 2018
ISBN 978-0-8020-7628-1 (paper)

♻

Printed on recycled paper

Canadian Cataloguing in Publication Data

Main entry under title:

Taxation and the distribution of income

(Research studies of the Fair Taxation Commission of Ontario)
Includes bibliographical references.
ISBN 978-0-8020-7628-1 (paper)

1. Tax incidence – Ontario.   2. Income distribution –
Ontario.   I. Block, Sheila.   II. Maslove, Allan M.,
1946–   .   III. Ontario.   Fair Tax Commission.
IV. Series.

HJ2323.T38 1994   336.2'94'09713   C94-932130-3

Contents

3 A Profile of High-Income Ontarians
BRIAN MURPHY, ROSS FINNIE, AND MICHAEL WOLFSON   101

Foreword

The Ontario Fair Tax Commission was established to examine the province's tax system as an integrated whole and, in conjunction with its working groups, to analyse individual components of the system in detail.

It has been many years since the Ontario tax system was subjected to a comprehensive examination. However, a great deal of research on taxation has been undertaken over the past two decades. This work, based in several disciplines, has been both theoretical and applied, and in this context the research program of the Fair Tax Commission was formulated.

The research program has two broad purposes. The first is, of course, to support the deliberations of the commissioners. The second, more novel objective is to inform public discussions of tax matters so that the commission's formal and informal public consultations can be of maximum value. For this reason we have opted to publish volumes in the series of studies as they are ready, rather than holding them all until the commission has completed its work. While our approach is more difficult from a technical and administrative perspective, we believe that the benefits will justify our decision.

The research program seeks to synthesize the existing published work on taxation; to investigate the implications for Ontario of the general research work; and, where required, to conduct original research on the context and principles for tax reform and on specific tax questions. We thus hope to add to the existing body of knowledge without duplicating it. The studies included in these publications are those that we believe make a contribution to the literature on taxation.

I would like to extend my thanks to my fellow commissioners and to the members of the FTC secretariat. I also thank the many members of the working groups and the advisory groups who have contributed to the research program and to the overall work of the commission.

Monica Townson, Chair

Introduction

Tax fairness is conventionally assessed in terms of the relationship of tax payments to incomes. The literature on taxation refers to two dimensions of equity – horizontal and vertical – both of which use income as the standard against which to measure tax liabilities. The first paper in this volume reports on the results of a general tax incidence analysis conducted for the Fair Tax Commission. It provides a picture of the overall relationship between taxation and incomes for Ontario residents, the baseline information necessary to form judgments about the vertical and horizontal equity properties of the current tax system. The following two papers focus on the lowest- and highest-income recipients, respectively, thereby providing a clearer picture of the circumstances of the two extremes of the income spectrum.

The study by Sheila Block and Richard Shillington provides a quantitative picture of the incidence of all taxes paid by Ontario residents. It thus updates earlier incidence studies and takes into account changes in received theory about the incidence of various taxes, and uses the new Statistics Canada Social Policy Simulation Database and Model (SPSD/M), which permits the calculation of incidence estimates at the household level. This study reviews the main theoretical conclusions on tax incidence and quantifies them in the form of a standard-case scenario and alternatives for the purpose of sensitivity testing. The sensitivity scenarios are based on varying assumptions about the inter-jurisdictional mobility of tax bases; it is this variation that seems to be the most critical factor in alternative incidence patterns.

Ken Battle and Sherri Torjman focus exclusively on the low end of income distribution and, in particular, on the interface between the income tax and transfer systems faced by social assistance recipients who supplement their benefits by working. For this paper, the authors constructed the Caledon Tax/Transfer Model, which allows them to quantify the marginal tax rates faced by a wide variety of household types in Ontario. The overall marginal "tax rate" that these households confront includes direct income taxes, tax credit reductions, payroll taxes, and social assistance benefit reduction rates. They find that the aggregate marginal tax rate faced by these households is punishingly high, and that the welfare benefit reduction (taxback) is, by far, the most important contributor to this "welfare wall." Battle and Torjman explore a number of alternative reform directions to facilitate the movement of social assistance recipients into the labour force. While easing the welfare taxback is obviously key, better integration with the explicit tax system is also important.

The paper by Brian Murphy, Ross Finnie, and Michael Wolfson sheds light on a segment of the population – the uppermost tail of the income distribution – that, curiously enough, has not been subjected to much empirical research in tax studies. Focusing on the top 5 per cent, 1 per cent, and 0.1 per cent of the income spectrum, Murphy, Finnie, and Wolfson describe the patterns of income and taxes and, to a lesser extent, the demographic profile of the high-income population. Their analysis shows that while the high-income earners face higher effective tax rates on average – reflecting the progressive income tax – a greater proportion of this group faces low effective tax rates – 10 per cent, or less than tax filers at lower income levels.

Together, the papers in this volume make a significant contribution to our understanding of the relationships between income and taxation for the Ontario population in general, and for individuals and households at the extremes of the income spectrum.

Allan M. Maslove

Taxation and the Distribution of Income

1 Incidence of Taxes in Ontario in 1991

SHEILA BLOCK and RICHARD SHILLINGTON

Introduction

Everyone pays taxes. An important part of judging the fairness of the taxes people pay is to determine how their taxes are related to their incomes and economic status. The relationship between income and taxes paid is a commonly accepted indicator of tax fairness both in the academic literature and in popular perceptions. While there are disagreements about what the ideal relationship between taxes and income should be, there is no real dispute that tax paid as a proportion of income is a meaningful measure of tax fairness.

Unfortunately, determining the amount of taxes paid by an individual or a household is not straightforward; neither is the measurement of income as obvious as it might seem at first thought. The taxes that people actually remit to governments often are different from the taxes they actually pay in an economic sense. The incomes that people receive in money terms may not be the same as their total economic income – the value of the goods and services over which they have control.

There are two interrelated reasons why determining who pays taxes is complex. First, many taxes are levied on and paid by organizations such as corporations, unincorporated businesses, and non-profit organizations. In the final analysis, it is necessary to attribute these taxes to people, and that requires the development of theories or hypotheses about how the taxes are distributed among the individuals who are associated with the organizations as owners (or asset holders more generally), employees, and clients. Second, when taxes are imposed they create incentives for individuals to change the economic decisions they make both personally and as decision-makers on behalf of organizations. These behavioural changes may relate to availability for work (labour supply), investment, consumption-saving choices, and decisions with respect to the purchase or sale of a wide range of specific goods and services.

All these changes in the behaviour of individuals and organizations have impacts on markets, resulting in changes in prices, wages, and rates of return. For example, a property tax imposed on rental units may result in tenants paying a higher rent than would otherwise have been the case. In this sense, we can say that the tax, which is imposed in the first instance on the landlord, is passed forward or *shifted* to the consumer of the product (the tenant) in the form of higher rents, and it is the tenant who ultimately pays the tax in economic terms. This determination of where the tax ultimately rests is called the *incidence* of the tax. Similarly, a tax imposed on the profits of a corporation may lead it to change its level of output, its pricing behaviour, and the amounts of inputs it uses (including capital). The final incidence of the tax may be partially on the corporation's shareholders, who receive lower returns than they otherwise would; the employees, who receive lower wages than they otherwise would; or the purchasers of its output, who pay higher prices than they otherwise would.

Obviously, reasonable people can reach different conclusions about how a tax is shifted and about its final incidence, depending on what they believe about the types of behavioural change that may be induced by the tax and about how markets operate. For this reason, analyses to determine the incidence of taxes can be quite contentious. Indeed, there are extensive debates in the economics literature about incidence studies in general, and about the incidence of particular taxes. Therefore, one must be careful not to read too much into the results of any one study, nor to attribute much significance to small differences. Nevertheless, as we shall see, a fairly broad range of assumptions about incidence and shifting generates quite similar results. To the extent that this is true, we can be confident that we are able to capture the general patterns of taxes that individuals pay relative to their incomes.

The shifting assumptions used in this study are based on the neo-classical economic literature. The estimates therefore generally reflect economic impacts in competitive markets that have reached a state of long-run equilibrium. These assumptions were chosen for two reasons. The first was a lack of literature outside the existing neoclassical framework, and therefore a dearth of alternative assumptions about the incidence of taxes outside this framework. The second was a desire to produce estimates that were within the parameters of the existing literature. The Canadian tax incidence literature is quite extensive. Some tax incidence estimates were produced in the context of full fiscal incidence studies: Gillespie (1980); Dodge (1975); Ruggeri, Van Wart, and Howard (1993). Other studies have estimated tax incidence alone, both in an annual framework – Goffman (1962); Maslove (1972); Whalley (1984); and Vermaeten, Gillespie, and Vermaeten (1994) – and in a lifetime framework – Davies, St. Hilaire, and Whalley (1984).

This study is an important component of the work of the Fair Tax Commission. The last comprehensive Ontario tax incidence study was completed for the Ontario Commission on Taxation (Johnson 1968). Estimates of the incidence of individual taxes as well as the tax system as a whole are an important indicator of the fairness of the current system. These estimates provide information on the impact of the current tax system on Ontarians' economic well-being, variations in tax burdens across income groups, and the regressive and progressive elements of the current tax system. These estimates can also provide information on the distributional impact of various policy changes.

This paper is structured in the following manner. The following section outlines various methodological issues. The third section then describes the shifting assumptions, data, and methodology used in this study. The final section discusses the empirical results of the study. The appendices provide information in tables and charts.

Methodology

The method used to estimate incidence is usually, and is in this paper, something of an accounting exercise. Incidence estimates for federal, provincial, and local taxes paid by Ontarians are based on a separate calculation for each tax that distributes the tax across income ranges. To construct these estimates, shifting assumptions are made for each tax. Based on these assumptions, taxes are allocated among the population according to various distributive series, such as income from wages and salaries. The process is repeated for each tax. When these estimates are added together, they yield an average total tax rate for each income range and/or demographic category. It should be noted that shifting assumptions are not statistically estimated, and are not tested. They are based on theoretical assumptions and conclusions from the literature.

In an incidence study of this kind three important choices have

6 Sheila Block and Richard Shillington

to be made: the shifting assumptions, the income concepts, and the time horizon. Each of these choices is subject to debate in the literature. The choices of income concept and time period are outlined below. The range of shifting assumptions in the literature and the economic conditions they describe are reviewed briefly in the next section. A standard model has been developed that, in our view, best categorizes the economy of Ontario. However, different assumptions are used in alternative models to provide some sensitivity analysis.

Purpose of Tax Incidence Studies

Full fiscal incidence estimates the effect of taxes, transfers, and expenditures on households by income classes. The purpose of these studies is to quantify the extent and direction of redistribution accomplished by the entire public sector. There is a debate in the literature about how accurately these studies can capture the impact of government on income distribution. Much of the criticism of these studies arises from the difficulties in the estimation of pre-government distributions of income (Dahlby 1985, 113–14). Tax incidence is a sub-category of full fiscal incidence, which quantifies the impact of the tax system in relation to the distribution of income.

Similar difficulties arise in determining the scenario used as background for tax incidence studies. If a pre-government measure of income is used, then the distributional impact of government expenditures must be addressed. If the analysis is based on a scenario of an economy with government, then a number of other assumptions must be made. If all other taxes and government expenditures are held constant while the tax being analysed is increased, then the analysis is absolute tax incidence. However, the attendant changes in the budgetary deficit or surplus will have an economic impact that will ultimately have a distributional impact. Another approach – "balanced budget incidence" – assumes that government expenditures are increased by the same amount as the revenue collected. Different assumptions about the pattern of the increase in expenditures yield different incidence results. Differential incidence studies, such as this one, compare the current tax mix to a proportional income tax. As a result, this study estimates the distributional consequences of the mix of taxes that is used to finance a given level of government expenditures.

Time Period: Lifetime vs. Annual Incidence

In estimates of tax incidence, a choice must be made as to the appropriate time period for measurement. This choice is determined by judgments on which period is the best measure of economic well-being. While traditionally this has been considered to be a year, more recently a lifetime has been proposed as a better measure. Proponents of lifetime tax incidence suggest that individuals have long time horizons over which they make their economic decisions. Estimates on a lifetime basis therefore provide a more accurate view of the distributional effects of the tax system. It is argued that the tax system has different impacts on individuals at different points in their life cycle (Fullerton and Rogers 1991). These different impacts arise from the changes over a lifetime of both income and expenditure patterns. Therefore, to obtain an accurate indication of the impact of the tax system on an individual, it is argued that a lifetime framework is needed. Intellectual support for longer time horizons in economic decision-making can be found in lifetime consumption theories (Ando and Modigliani 1963; and Friedman 1957).[1] These theories suggest that individuals' consumption decisions and conceptions of well-being are related not to current income but to longer-term income flows. Support for this view can be found in the fact that spending patterns can be explained by these long-term income flows more successfully than by current income. Individuals and families purchasing major assets such as housing generally make such commitments with their long-run income prospects in mind. In addition, individuals who invest in their own human capital are clearly acting in terms of a long-term plan and not simply in terms of current considerations.

The argument for annual incidence begins with a recognition that individuals do take into account long-term considerations when making important decisions, though whether this long term is truly a lifetime perspective is less clear. However, long-term income prospects can only be contemplated with a high level of uncertainty. The possibility of unforeseen income declines, bouts of unemployment, major illness, and the like, make planning based on assumed future income flows uncertain. In addition, private contracts, to which most individuals' incomes are related, are of relatively short duration, perhaps extending for several years but much less than a lifetime. Even if individuals did have lifetime planning horizons, institutions, in particular financial markets, do not accommodate them. Transactions costs and the cost of information result in differences in the treatment of human and physical capital by financial institutions. Because of these capital market imperfections, current economic well-being is dependent on current income as well as future income.

Perhaps more to the point, lifetime incidence estimates assume a policy environment that does not in fact exist. First and foremost, the tax system itself is not fixed. Changes in tax regimes that affect net incomes and wealth positions are far from uncommon. Second, the collection of services that individuals may receive from government at various times, and that affect their incomes, is certainly not fixed. Third, most other public programs are structured in frameworks much shorter than lifetimes. For example, programs such as UI and social assistance adopt frameworks defined in terms of weeks. Finally, annual cycles are the standard time horizons for most public- and private-sector transactions, including such things as tax administration, labour agreements, and other contracts.

Individuals and families are clearly cognizant of long-term horizons. However, given the considerations noted above, it is also clear that short-term positions (for which a year is a reasonable practical measure) are central to individual decisions and to perceptions of well-being. Therefore, annual incidence measures are valid estimates of tax distributions and more relevant to households than lifetime measures.[2]

However, these arguments for annual frameworks do not address concerns about the differential impact of the tax system at various points in the life cycle. Generally, incomes rise during early years, level off during later working years, and fall during retirement. Individuals of different ages consume different goods, receive income from different sources, and as a result pay different amounts of annual taxes. Many of the questions raised about the impact of changes in income and expenditure patterns over a lifetime can be answered without moving to a lifetime framework. This can be done through incidence estimates be demographic groups. This will highlight the differences in incidence among different family types and age groups.

Income Measures

There are two broad approaches to the measurement of income that can be used in fiscal incidence studies. The first of these is "pre-fisc" income, which attempts to measure pre-government income. This measurement of income begins with money income less transfers and includes: wages and salaries, self-employment income, and income from capital. In order to come closer to a Haig-Simons concept of command over economic resources, various accrual items are added:

imputed income from owner-occupied housing, retained corporate earnings, accrued capital gains, and interest earned on life insurance policies and savings. This measure is then adjusted to construct a measure of hypothetical income that removes the impact of government. First, all taxes that are assumed to be shifted to sources of income (e.g., labour, capital) are added back into income. For example, the portion of corporate taxes that are assumed to be shifted onto capital and the employer-paid portion of social security taxes that are assumed to be shifted to labour income are added to those sources of income.

The second approach is "post-fisc" income, which attempts to measure post-government income. This measure of income includes transfers and the value of government expenditures. Taxes are subtracted from income. "Post-fisc" income can only be estimated in the context of a full fiscal incidence study, as the benefits from government expenditures have to be distributed to people or households according to some rationale or assumptions. Pre- and post-fisc incomes are the parameters for the choice of income measures, and a number of variations within these two choices have been used in the literature.

This study uses a broad income measure, which includes pre-fisc income plus transfers. This measure of income is used because it is the most appropriate for policy analysis, as it is the income that households control. While pre-fisc income excludes transfers that are under households' control, post-fisc income includes the benefits from other government expenditures, which households control only very indirectly. Of the income measures used for incidence analysis, this one most closely resembles what individuals consider to be their income. More practically, in the absence of a full fiscal incidence analysis, the distribution of government expenditures on goods and services was not available.

The choice of income concepts has an impact on the apparent progressivity or regressivity of the resulting incidence estimates (Whalley 1984, 671). Because of the impact of transfers and government expenditures, pre-fisc income results in a more regressive incidence pattern than does post-fisc income. In addition, the income measures change with changes in shifting assumptions. Comparisons of the impact of different shifting assumptions include the impact on the change in tax payable and on income.

Shifting Assumptions

Taxes can have an impact on households through their sources of income, their uses of income, and through their wealth holdings. The sources of income are capital (including land) and labour. Uses of income are the savings and expenditure of households. Wealth holdings include principal residences, financial assets, and a range of other assets. Incidence focuses on the relative effects of changes in income resulting from a change in taxation. If the effect is on the uses side, there is a change in relative prices of goods and services consumed by households.[3] If the effect is on the sources side, it is a change in the relative prices paid to the various sources of income. Because sources and uses vary by income ranges, these shifting assumptions determine the progressivity or regressivity of the results.

Probably the contentious issues in the literature on tax incidence are the shifting assumptions – especially those relating to corporate, property, and sales and excise taxes. For corporate taxes, the debate is whether the tax is borne by owners of corporate capital or whether it is shifted to owners of other forms of capital: to labour or to consumers. The appropriate shifting assumption depends, in part, on the openness of the economy. For property taxes, the debate centres on the appropriate shifting assumption for the portion of the tax that falls on the structures. Differences in assumptions depend largely on differences in assumptions about the mobility of capital invested in housing or other uses. The debate on consumption taxes is whether they should be distributed according to consumption or according to factor payments. Stronger consensus exists in the literature relating to other taxes. Income taxes are generally assumed not to be shifted. Payroll taxes are generally treated as a tax on labour. The range of assumptions used in the literature and those used in the standard case are discussed below.

Income and Payroll Taxes

In the literature, the personal income tax is always treated as paid by income recipients.[4] The shifting assumptions for social security contributions and payroll taxes have been subject to less debate than those for some other taxes. Incidence studies in the United States and Canada have treated employee contributions consistently as a tax on labour, and the majority of these studies treat the employer portion of these taxes as a tax on labour as well (Dahlby 1985, 130–1; Whalley 1984, 158–9). The supply of labour must be inelastic for this to occur, or the supply of capital must be completely elastic. Dahlby provides an exhaustive review of the theory and empirical evidence on the shifting of these kinds of taxes. He concludes that, in the long run, labour bears over 80 per cent of employer payroll taxes (Dahlby 1993, 57).

Corporate Taxes

Incidence studies have allocated corporate income tax to corporate shareholders, to owners of all forms of capital, and to a combination of owners of capital and consumers or labour (Dahlby 1985, 130–1; Whalley 1984, 158–9). Assumptions about the incidence of corporate taxes depend on structure of markets, including their competitiveness and the openness of the economy.

In a competitive, closed economy model with fixed stocks of factors and mobility of factors between uses in the economy, all forms of capital income will bear the burden of the tax (Musgrave, Musgrave, and Bird 1987, 384–5). Mobility of factors between different uses results in the burden of a sector-specific tax on a factor affecting that factor equally outside and inside the taxed sector. As a result, the taxation of corporate capital will result in a reduced rate of return for all other forms of capital as well. This is because capital moves out of the taxed sector into the untaxed sector until rates of return are equalized. This longer-run result is appropriate because incidence estimates are concerned with the long run, when all adjustments have occurred. In the short run, in a competitive market, the impact of the tax will be to reduce the rate of return on corporate capital. Corporate taxes appear to be more progressive if it is assumed that they are borne by capital income specific to taxed industries rather than capital income in general, because the latter includes widely held housing capital.

In his 1980 study, Gillespie allocated half of the corporate income tax (CIT) burden to capital in general, and the other half to holders of corporate equity (Whalley 1984, 659). This is probably due to the assumption that, in the short run, there is some departure from a long-run sharing of CIT burdens among all capital owners. Pechman and Okner (1974) assumed that only part of the corporate tax is on capital income and part is shifted forward (Whalley 1984, 659). A number of market situations can result in shifting of the tax. Under some labour market conditions the tax burden can be passed back to labour (Musgrave, Musgrave, and Bird 1987, 386–9).

However, an open-economy context results in a very different, shifting pattern. A small, open economy facing world rates of return for capital and world prices for its products, in the presence of foreign tax credits, can result in the following shifting pattern. The rate of return to capital is net of an international tax rate. As a result, corporate taxes up to the international level are borne by capital. Domestic taxes above this level are shifted either forward to consumers or backward to

labour. Ontario is a subnational jurisdiction in an economy that is open
to international and interprovincial trade and capital movements. It
can be argued that this is the incidence assumption that best describes
the province's economic conditions. This is the assumption used in the
standard case for public corporations.

Tax revenue from Canadian-controlled private corporations
(CCPCs) is assumed to be distributed differently from those of public
corporations. In particular, capital invested in these corporations is
assumed to be less mobile. This is particularly true for owner-operated
CCPCs. The likelihood of the capital in these CCPCs being moved to
another asset is lower due to the investment of the owners' time and
expertise in the firms. The integration of the personal and corporate
income tax systems, through the dividend gross-up and tax credits
system, is designed to levy the same tax whether the income is earned
directly or through a corporation. The aim is tax neutrality between
self-employed income and CCPC income, suggesting that revenue
from CCPC income should be distributed in the same manner as personal income taxes are.

Property Taxes

A conceptual distinction is usually made between the property tax
paid on the value of land and that paid on the value of structures. The
supply of land is considered fixed and immobile; the supply of structures or improvements is like any other form of capital. While the
portion of property taxes is assumed to remain with the owner of the
land, the portion on structures is assumed to be shifted to capital
income, or to be shifted to residential rents and consumers (Dahlby
1985, 130–1; Whalley 1984, 158–9).

There are two approaches to property tax incidence in the literature
(Bird and Slack 1978, 36–53). The traditional view assumes that the
supply of land is fixed, and consequently that the part of the property
tax that falls on land must be borne by landowners. This portion of the
property tax is therefore capitalized into the price of the land. The
supply of structures, on the other hand, may be altered in the long run.
The flexibility in the supply of structures results in the property tax on
structures being entirely shifted forward to the users of property. For
rented residential properties, this results in higher prices to tenants. In
the case of property taxes on business structures, the increase in occupancy costs, in turn, results in higher prices to consumers. Owner-

occupiers of residential property bear the tax on structures and on land. Owner-occupiers bear the tax on land in the guise of owners and bear the tax on structures as consumers of housing services.

The new view of property tax incidence treats the portion of the tax on land in the same manner as the traditional view. However, the property tax on structures is treated as a tax on capital assets. A tax on a particular type of capital is analytically similar to a tax on capital in a particular sector, and so the competitive model outlined above would suggest that the component of the tax on structures borne by capital is shared equally by owners of all forms of capital. The tax reduces the rate of return to all capital.

An intermediate case has been developed that takes into account less flexibility in the supply of structures in the short run. It also assumes greater sensitivity of the demand for housing to changes in price. This case, like the others, assumes that the supply of land is fixed. These conditions result in some of the property tax on structures being shifted forward to consumers and renters and some of it being shifted backward to capital owners.

An open-economy context with an international rate of return on capital and world prices for products results in a different pattern of tax shifting (Ruggeri, Van Wart, and Howard 1993, 37–8). The supply of land remains fixed and there is no change in treatment. There is a change in the treatment of residential rental property and commercial and industrial property. Since residential rental property is not a traded good, the tax on structures is fully shifted forward to renters. The industrial and commercial property tax on structures paid by industries producing traded goods and services cannot be passed forward in higher prices or remain on capital. In this situation, taxes on structures would reduce the rate of return to capital resulting in a reduction in the supply. This reduction in the supply of capital would result in a decrease in demand for labour. As a result, the tax burden would be shifted back to labour. For non-traded industries it could be expected that the tax would be passed on to consumers. These assumptions are used in the standard case.

Consumption Taxes

While most incidence studies assume that consumers bear the cost of consumption taxes in proportion to their purchases of taxable goods, some studies distribute the tax burden according to factor payments.

The shifting assumptions about sales taxes are particularly important, as these taxes account for a large enough share of total revenue to affect the overall distributive pattern of the tax system.

The view that the incidence of a broad-based consumption tax is on consumers arises from the analysis of a competitive model of the economy (Musgrave 1959, 372–7). A consumption tax in this framework affects uses rather than sources of income. The imposition of a consumption tax increases the return from savings, and decreases the amount of consumption obtained from current income. The impact of the tax depends on the amount of income that is saved. The higher the savings rate of the household, the lower the burden of this form of taxation. This is the assumption used on the standard case.

An alternative view is that consumers bear the expense of sales taxes in proportion to the share of their income that comes from factor payments (Browning 1978). On the assumption that government transfer payments are indexed to increases in the consumer price index (CPI), an increase in consumption taxes will have a different impact on households who receive their income from transfer payments as compared with those who receive their income from factor payments. The impact of the tax on households who receive their income from transfer payments will be offset by indexation, while those who derive their income from factor payments will see the real value of their income reduced by the full increase in the tax (Whalley 1984, 158–9).

There are a number of critiques of the Browning approach.[5] The assumption that transfer payments are fully indexed is one that is immediately apparent. To address this problem, a method of measuring the degree of indexation and incorporating it into tax incidence estimates has been developed (Ruggeri and Bluck 1992). However, this method does not address the more fundamental problems associated with this assumption. Because indexing affects the absolute price level, while incidence studies are concerned with relative prices, the introduction of changes in the price level to an incidence study can be considered inappropriate. This approach does not take into account that, regardless of the sources of income, consumers are worse off than savers in the presence of a consumption tax. When the indexation of transfer payments is introduced to a tax incidence study, one element of expenditure incidence is arbitrarily introduced into the estimates. Finally, some factor payments are effectively indexed, such as wages with cost-of-living allowance (COLA) clauses and nominal interest rates.

While we do not accept the Browning approach for these reasons, an assumption that produces an incidence pattern somewhat similar to that of Browning's results is used as a sensitivity test (see below).

Budget Balance

The assumptions underlying tax incidence studies are based on a balanced-budget framework. The presence of a deficit results in the provision of public services that will have to be paid for later. In full fiscal incidence studies, which attempt to distribute both the benefits and costs of government activity, this presents more of a problem than in tax incidence studies. There are a couple of possible approaches to deficit financing that are available. It can be treated as a current liability using a Ricardian equivalence approach,[6] or it can be treated as a future tax liability, and therefore considered irrelevant to an annual incidence study (Ruggeri, Van Wart, and Howard 1993, 6). If the deficit is treated as a current liability, assumptions must be made on how to distribute it among the various tax bases. These assumptions have an impact on the incidence results. Alternatively, treating the deficit as a future tax liability can be considered to underestimate the tax burden. Given the context of a tax incidence rather than a full fiscal incidence study, and the impact on the results of distributing government deficits, they are treated as a future liability in this paper.

Assumptions Used in This Study

Income Measures

The income concept used in this study is the broad income measure, which includes pre-fisc income and transfers. It includes: factor incomes gross of personal income tax; transfer payments; imputed rent from owner-occupied housing; interest accruing on private pension funds and life insurance funds; retained earnings; and capital gains from principal residences. Refundable tax credits, such as the GST tax credit and the Ontario sales and property tax credits can be considered analytically equivalent to transfer payments, which are delivered through the tax system. They are therefore treated as transfer payments and included in income rather than treated as reductions in tax payable.[7] Corporate taxes is added back into capital income, as are the portion of property taxes that fall on capital. In addition, the employer portion of payroll taxes is added back into wages and salaries, as are consumption taxes when they are shifted onto this source of income.

Shifting Assumptions

Given the debate in the literature, a choice had to be made on the most appropriate set of shifting assumptions for a standard case. This required judgment on what set of assumptions were most reasonable for Ontario in 1991. The most salient characteristics of the Ontario economy were deemed to be the province's status as a subnational jurisdiction and as a small, open economy. The increased internation-alization of markets, and in particular capital markets, is also a critical characteristic in choosing the appropriate shifting assumptions. These characteristics, in combination with an assumption of internationally mobile capital, shaped the standard case. The standard case incorpo-rates our judgment on the level of this mobility and its impact on the shifting assumptions.

Three alternative scenarios were also developed. These attempted to capture the range of shifting assumptions in the literature set in the context of varying degrees of factor mobility. These cases are useful for sensitivity analysis to determine the impact of different shifting assumptions on incidence results.

Standard Incidence Scenario

- Corporate taxes paid on income or capital from Canadian-controlled private corporations (CCPCs) are distributed differently from taxa-tion of other corporations. Taxation of CCPC income is distributed according to personal income tax payments, while the remainder of corporate income tax revenues is distributed as described below.
- The amount of capital and corporate income tax paid that is equal to the international tax rate is shifted to all forms of capital income; capital and corporate income taxes above that amount are shifted in the following manner: half to wages and salaries and half to con-sumption.
- Personal income taxes are borne by the taxpayer.
- The amount of property taxes on structures (that is, not on owner-occupied property) equal to the international average is shifted to all capital income. This reflects the view that a tax on a particular type of capital will affect all owners of capital, due to its mobility between uses. Property taxes above this amount are shifted to occu-pants in the case of residential real estate, and split between labour and consumers in proportion to the traded and non-traded sectors of the economy for commercial and industrial properties.

- Property taxes on land are not shifted, and remain with landowners.
- Sales and excise taxes (including the indirect portion of the retail sales tax) are borne by consumers of taxed goods.
- Eighty per cent of payroll taxes – Canada Pension Plan, Unemployment Insurance, Employer Health Tax, Workers' Compensation – are shifted to employees; the other 20 per cent is shifted to all forms of capital income.

More Mobile I Scenario

This model incorporates some assumptions that can be associated with higher levels of mobility than represented in our standard case. In particular, international price setting for consumption goods is assumed to occur more frequently. The following assumptions were changed from those in the standard model:

- Consumption is assumed to be more mobile than in the standard model. As a result, the indirect component of the Ontario retail sales tax is shifted to labour.
- Commercial and industrial property taxes on structures are shifted fully to labour, and taxes on residential rental property are shifted to occupants.
- All payroll taxes are shifted to employees.

More Mobile II Scenario

In this model, an increased share of consumption taxes were shifted to a factor income. The following assumption was changed from those in the more mobile I model:

- Consumption is assumed to be more mobile. Freer trade patterns mean that prices of consumer goods are set in international markets, similar to price setting of capital in the standard model. As a result, sales and excise taxes are shifted to wages and salaries. This is due to labour being the least mobile factor of production.

One might argue that an assumption more consistent with the arguments in this paper would be that sales and excise taxes up to the international rate would be borne by domestic consumers and only the differential would be shifted backwards to labour. Our assumption, being more extreme, provides an "outer envelope" estimate of tax incidence for the highest mobility scenario.

Less Mobile Scenario

In this model, the shifting assumptions that could be associated with less internationalization of markets were used. In these assumptions, capital is less mobile, both between different uses and between jurisdictions. The following assumptions were changed from those in the standard model:

- Corporate income and capital taxes on companies that are not CCPCs fall half on dividends, half on consumption. This reflects an assumption that capital is less mobile, both between different uses in Ontario and between jurisdictions.
- Property taxes on structures for rental accommodation are shifted half to renters; half is not shifted and is borne by landlords. For owner-occupied dwellings these taxes are not shifted; for commercial and industrial properties the tax is shifted to domestic consumers.

Appendix 1 shows the detailed distributive series used for distributing income and taxes to households.

Quantification of Assumptions

Corporate Tax

The treatment of corporate income and capital taxes outlined above operates on the assumption that from a Canadian or Ontario perspective (i.e., a "small" participant in the global capital market) the world price for capital is fixed. The U.S. rate is used as a proxy for the world rate. Estimates of marginal effective tax rates are used.[8] It can be argued that it is differences in marginal rates that trigger capital mobility decisions. Ontario estimates for 1991 are available from a paper produced for the Fair Tax Commission by Chen and Mintz (1993). Estimates for the United States are available for 1990, produced by McKenzie and Mintz.

The McKenzie and Mintz estimates are only calculated for large and medium-sized businesses. They are for fully tax-paying firms, in an environment without risk. Under these assumptions, their estimate for the U.S. rate is 20.4 per cent for 1990 (McKenzie and Mintz 1990, table 2).

The Chen and Mintz estimates include both capital and corporate income taxes. Only fully taxable firms with riskless investment are considered. The results, including capital taxes and excluding the mining industry, show that the combined aggregate effective marginal tax rate for large Ontario firms is 30.2 (Chen and Mintz 1993, table 5, 18).[9]

Property Tax

The shifting assumptions in the literature about property taxes require that tax on land be separated out from tax on structures. The residential property tax must be split between rental accommodation and owner-occupied dwellings. Finally, taxes on commercial and residential properties must also be separated. The latter information was available from the Ontario Ministry of Municipal Affairs. Data on the first two splits are not available. The residential split between owner-occupied and rented structures is usually assumed to be 67 to 33. Usually a 25-per-cent-for-land–75-per-cent-for-structures split is assumed (Kitchen 1992, 51). In addition, the measures used above for corporate taxes are used to determine the shares of property tax on structures that fall on capital income as opposed to consumption and rent in the more mobile models.

Data Sources and Estimation Methods

The SPSD/M model was used as the source for data on the 1991 tax and transfer system in Ontario, and for the distribution of income by source and for the distribution of expenditures.[10] For these micro data, the base 1986 data were adjusted to estimate 1991 values. The inflation factors were selected to yield reasonable 1991 average family incomes for Ontario. The income tax and consumption tax structure and rates were based on the tax structure in place in Ontario in 1991.

The analysis of the results is at the household level.[11] A household may include more than one census family. Thus a high-income household may include a lower-income individual or family that may in fact collect certain targeted tax credits. It should be noted that average household incomes are about 10 per cent higher than average family incomes.

Data on a national accounts basis are used to estimate income, transfers, and tax burden in Ontario. The source for the income data (other than government transfers and pensions) was the Provincial Economic Accounts, developed by the Office of Economic Policy at the Ontario Ministry of Finance. Income on a national accounts basis does not include benefits from private pension plans. To obtain these data, Revenue Canada's 1989 *Taxation Statistics* grossed up to 1991 values, were used. The estimate for capital gains (or, as happened in the year in question, losses) on principal residences was derived from housing equity data from the 1986 Statistics Canada Family Expenditure Survey. The value of equity in homes was then updated using the Multiple Listing Service (MLS) price series for Ontario developed by the Canadian Real Estate Association. Unpublished data from Statistics Canada's Provincial Economic Accounts were used for both tax and transfer data.

An SPSD run provided data on the distribution of a number of variables by income (income items by type, estimated income taxes, estimated consumption taxes and expenditures on a range of personal items). These are used in the analysis to distribute the Provincial Accounts totals to households in various income groups. Different variables were used to distribute various income and tax items among income groups. Some of these variables differed among the various shifting assumptions.

Results

Total Tax Incidence

Figure 1 below shows total tax incidence for the standard case. Total tax incidence includes federal, provincial, and local taxes paid by Ontario households in 1991. The tax system is progressive over the first six decile groups. The average effective tax rate is 27.6 per cent in the first decile group rising to 39.8 per cent in the sixth decile group. The tax system is roughly proportional over the next four decile groups, with the average effective tax rate fluctuating around 40 per cent. In the tenth decile group, the average effective tax rate rises to 43.3 per cent.

Incidence by Level of Government

Figure 2 shows incidence estimates for federal, provincial, and local taxes in the standard case. Federal taxes show a steadily progressive profile over the first seven decile groups, with the average effective tax

FIGURE 1
Total Tax Incidence, Ontario Households, 1991
All Levels of Government

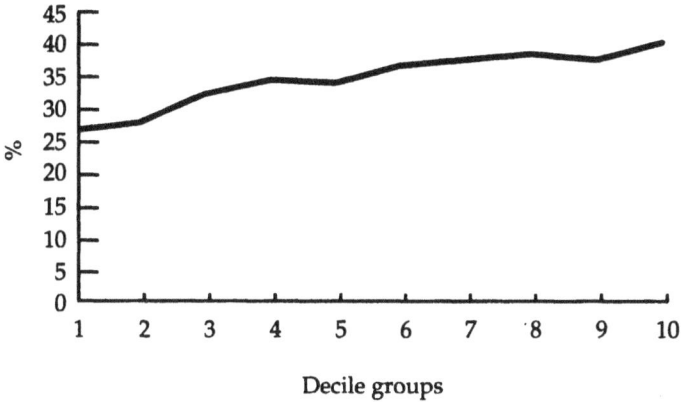

FIGURE 2
Incidence by Level of Government, Standard Case

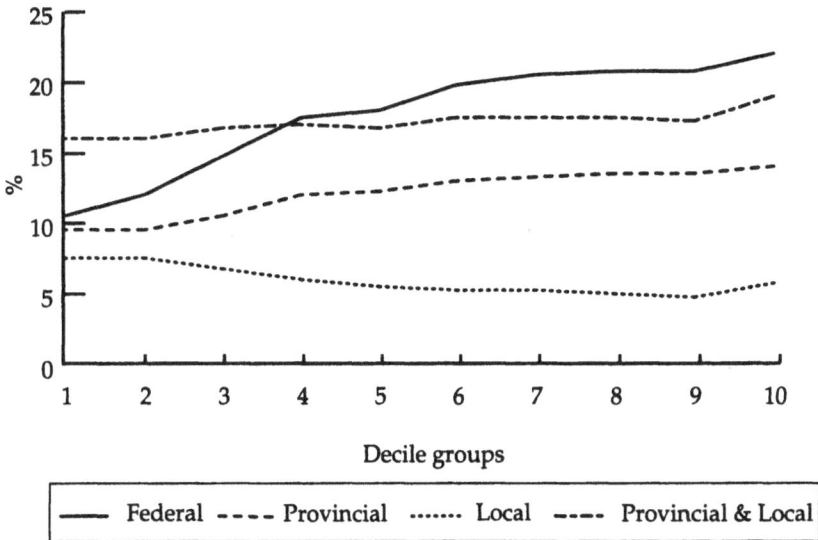

rate rising from 10.6 per cent in the first decile group to 21.7 per cent in the seventh decile group. Over the next three decile groups, federal taxes fluctuate around 22 per cent. Provincial and local taxes are roughly proportional over the first nine decile groups, fluctuating between 17.4 and 18.6 per cent. The average effective tax rate rises to 20.1 per cent in the tenth decile group. This is a combination of generally regressive local taxes and moderately progressive provincial taxes up to the sixth decile group. Local taxes are regressive over the first nine decile groups, with the average effective tax rate ranging from 7.4 per cent in the first decile group to 4.3 per cent in the ninth decile group, and averaging 5.3 per cent in the tenth decile group. Total provincial taxes are moderately progressive over the first six decile groups, ranging from 9.9 per cent to 13.6 per cent. The average effective provincial tax rate fluctuates around 14 per cent from the seventh to tenth decile groups.

Progressivity of Selected Tax Bases

Figure 3 shows the incidence of various taxes using the assumptions in the standard case. As would be expected, personal income taxes have the most progressive incidence pattern. The Ontario personal income tax is progressive across all income ranges. It is also the tax that accounts for the largest share of provincial revenues. Average effective tax rates vary from 0.2 per cent for households in the first decile group to 7.3 per cent for households in the tenth decile group. Ontario personal income taxes have a more progressive profile than federal personal income taxes. This is in part due to the combination of the Ontario tax reduction and Ontario's high income surtaxes.

The personal income tax is the only provincial tax with a progressive distributive pattern. Like other consumption taxes, the Ontario retail sales tax has a regressive profile. The average effective tax rate is 5.3 per cent in the first decile group dropping to 2.7 per cent in the tenth decile group. This tax is the second-largest source of revenue for the provincial government after personal income tax.

Residential and commercial and industrial property taxes show a generally regressive profile. Residential property taxes have a regressive profile over the first six decile groups, with average effective tax rates ranging from 4.4 to 2.3 per cent. Over the next three decile groups, the effective tax rate fluctuates around 2 per cent. Commercial and industrial property taxes do not show a clear pattern of incidence across income ranges. The combined impact of the retail sales tax and the property taxes almost directly offsets the progressivity of the per-

FIGURE 3
Distributive Pattern of Selected Ontario Tax Bases, Standard Case, 1991

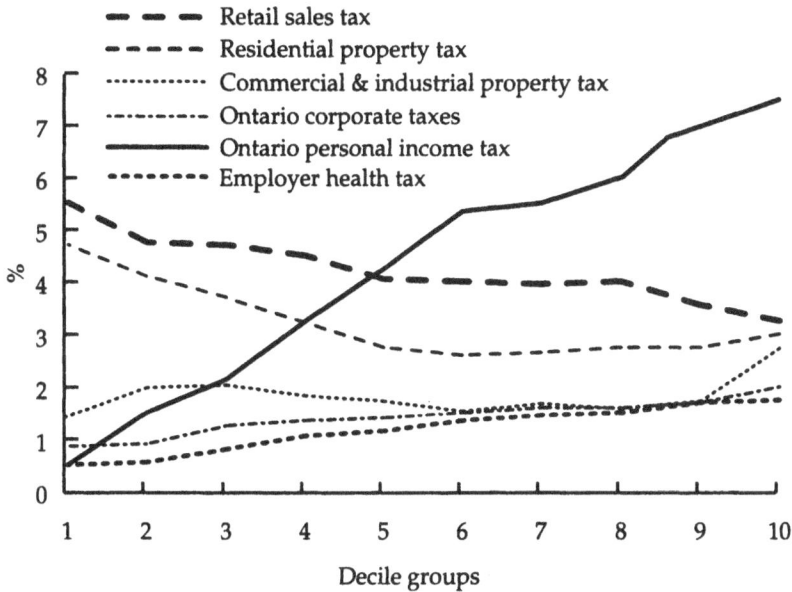

sonal income tax over the first nine deciles. This results in the proportionality of the combined provincial and local tax burden over the first nine decile groups.

Corporate taxes and the employer health tax account for smaller shares of total Ontario revenue. As a result, they have a minimal impact on the overall incidence results. The employer health tax has a progressive profile over the first six decile groups. The average effective tax rate is 0.2 per cent in the first decile group, rising to 1 per cent in the sixth decile group. It fluctuates around 1 per cent over the next three decile groups. In the context of internationally mobile capital, Ontario corporate taxes (on both income and capital) are roughly proportional. The average effective corporate tax rate fluctuates around 1 per cent across all income ranges.

Incidence Estimates by Family Type

The use of the SPSD/M model allows estimates of incidence by family type. The data series for the various income and expenditure items used to distribute income and taxes across income categories can be selected for various family types. However, small sample sizes for Ontario restricts the number of family types for which results can be reported.[12] This section reports results for three family types: couples with children, couples with at least one elderly person, and non-elderly couples without children. Due to small sample sizes, results are reported for income quintile groups.[13]

Incidence estimates by family are shown in figure 4. The incidence pattern for elderly couples is regressive over the first two quintile groups, and slightly progressive over the next three quintile groups. The average effective tax rate in the first quintile group is 37.2 per cent. It then drops off sharply to 32.1 in the second quintile group. Between the third and fifth quintile groups the average effective tax rate rises from 33.3 per cent to 35.5 per cent. Incidence estimates for two-parent families show a progressive profile, with the average effective tax rate in the first quintile group at 31.6 per cent, rising to 43.2 per cent in the fifth quintile group. The incidence pattern for non-elderly couples without children is generally progressive, with average effective tax rates ranging from 30.4 per cent in the first quintile group, levelling off at 42.8 per cent in the top two quintile groups.

Alternative Scenarios

Figure 5 shows total tax incidence for the four alternative scenarios. The incidence pattern in the less mobile case is virtually indistinguishable from the standard case. The average effective tax rate is 29.4 per cent in the first decile group for the less mobile case, rising to 40.1 per cent in the sixth decile group. Total tax incidence in this case is roughly proportional over the next three decile groups, with the average effective tax rate fluctuating around 40 per cent. In the tenth decile group the average effective tax rate rises to 43.2 per cent.

The overall pattern of incidence is also similar in the more mobile I case. In this case, the tax system is progressive over the first six decile groups The tax system is roughly proportional over the next four decile groups. Over the first three decile groups in the more mobile I case, the average effective tax rate is lower, by between 1 and 2 percentage points, than in the standard case. The reduced burden on these decile groups from consumption and industrial and commercial property taxes outweighs the increased burden from residential property taxes. In addition, because the portion of the retail sales tax shifted onto labour enters into the income measure in more mobile I, income is

FIGURE 4
Incidence Estimates by Family Type, Standard Case, 1991
All Taxes

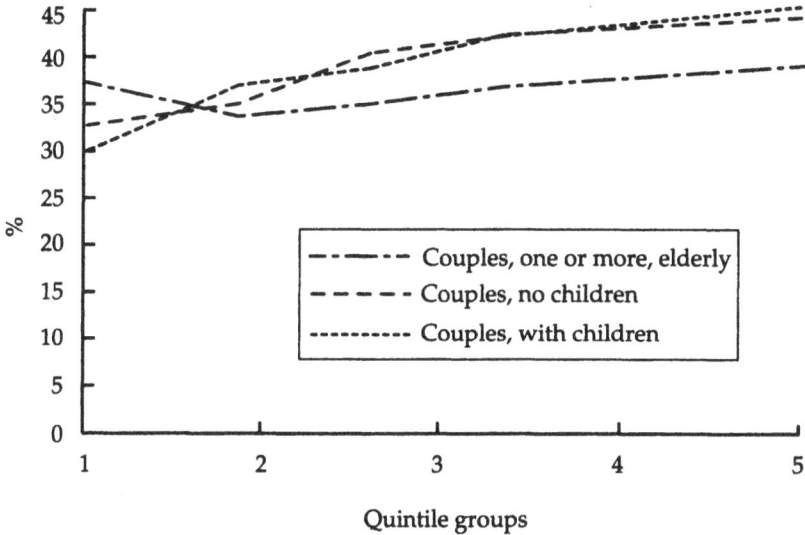

higher in this case. This results in the overall lower pattern of average effective tax rates.

The more mobile II case has a more progressive profile. This results from the assumption that the sales tax burden is shifted back onto labour income. Average effective tax rates range from 15.5 per cent in the first decile group to 40.6 per cent in the tenth decile group. All consumption taxes are added back into incomes to obtain a pre-tax income measure. Average incomes are therefore higher across all income ranges. This accounts for this case's average effective tax rates being below those of the standard case across income ranges.

Impact of Varying, Shifting Assumptions

The different cases varied the assumptions on property, consumption, and corporate tax shifting. Only the changes in the consumption tax shifting had an impact on the overall pattern of incidence. However, the impact on overall tax incidence is a combination of both the change

FIGURE 5
Distributive Patterns of Alternative Scenarios, Ontario Households, 1991
Total Tax Incidence

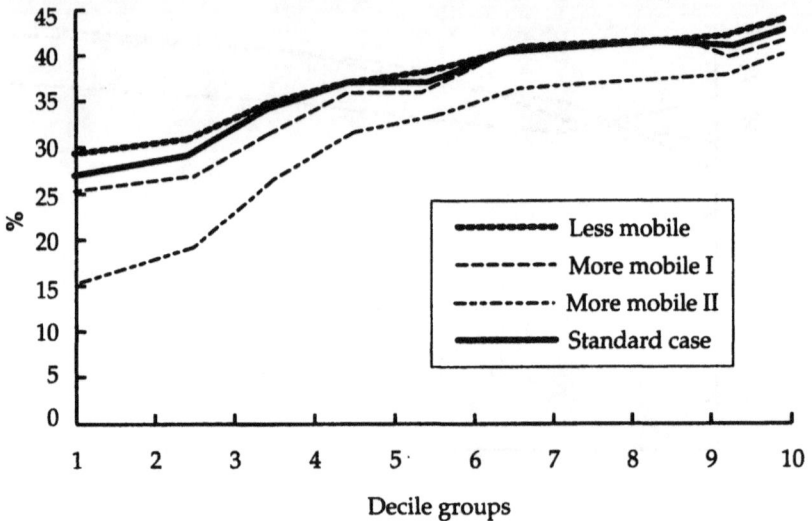

in incidence of the individual tax and the share of total revenue accounted for by that tax. This section will describe the impact of changing, shifting assumptions on the progressivity of various individual taxes.

Three different shifting assumptions are used for property taxes. In all cases, the property tax on land remains with owners (along with the tax on structures for owner-occupied residential property). In the standard case, the share of tax on structures that is equal to the international average is shifted to all forms of capital income. Property taxes above this amount are shifted to occupants in the case of residential real estate, and split between labour and consumers for commercial and industrial properties. In the more mobile cases, property taxes on structures on commercial and industrial property are shifted to labour and on residential rental property are shifted to occupants. In the less mobile case, property taxes on structures for rental accommodation are shifted half to renters; half is not shifted and is borne by landlords. For commercial and industrial properties the tax is shifted to domestic consumers.

Figure 6 shows the incidence patterns that result from varying the shifting assumptions for property taxes. In all three cases, total property taxes show a generally regressive profile over the first nine decile groups. However, the standard case is close to proportional over the first two decile groups, while the other two shifting assumptions result in a regressive pattern between these two decile groups. In all three cases property taxes are progressive between the ninth and tenth decile groups.

Two different shifting assumptions are used for taxes on income and capital taxes on corporations that are not CCPCs. In the standard and more mobile cases, the portion of corporate taxes that is equal to the U.S. average is shifted to capital income in general. Capital and corporate income taxes above that level of taxation are shifted half to wages and salaries and half to consumption. In the less mobile case, taxes on these corporations are split between consumption and dividends. In all cases, income from CCPCs is distributed as personal income taxes. This component of corporate taxes is therefore progressive.

Figure 7 shows the incidence patterns that result from varying the shifting assumptions on corporate taxes excluding CCPCS. In the standard case, average effective tax rates rise from 1.5 per cent in the first decile group to 3.3 per cent in the tenth decile group. In the less mobile case, the average effective tax rate fluctuates around 2.5 per cent. The two incidence patterns are virtually indistinguishable.

Three different shifting assumptions were used for consumption taxes. In the standard case, sales and excise taxes are borne by consumers of taxed goods. In the more mobile I case, the indirect component of the RST is shifted to labour. In the more mobile II case, sales and excise taxes are shifted on wages and salaries. These assumptions result in very different patterns of incidence.

Figure 8 shows the incidence patterns that result from varying the shifting assumptions on consumption taxes. When consumption taxes are shifted forward onto the consumption of the taxed good, these taxes have a regressive profile across all income ranges. In the more mobile I case, the overall profile remains regressive. In the more mobile II case, the tax is generally progressive up to the eighth decile group. The average effective tax rate is 2.3 per cent in the first decile group rising to 10.3 per cent in the eighth decile group, and falling off to 8.1 per cent in the tenth decile group.

However, as already noted, the main function of this aspect of the more mobile II scenario is to estimate the distribution resulting from

FIGURE 6
Impact of Varying Shifting Assumptions, Property Tax

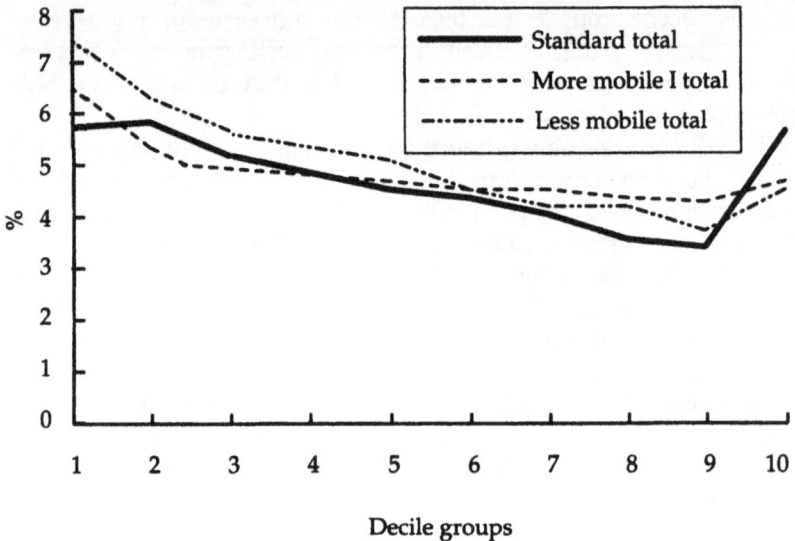

Decile groups

the most extreme shifting assumptions. The likelihood that this scenario represents the actual distribution is small.

Conclusion

The distribution of tax burdens that emerges from this study is quite clear. Overall, the tax system is progressive from the lowest income levels to about the sixth decile group. From then on the pattern is essentially proportional or flat relative to incomes. To express this slightly differently, progressivity ends at about $50,000 of household income. Provincial and local taxes viewed together show essentially a proportional pattern, the combined effect of regressive local-level taxes and mildly progressive (over the first six decile groups) or proportional provincial taxes.

The personal income tax is the only tax levied by the Ontario government that exhibits a clearly progressive pattern over the entire income spectrum. The other two major revenue sources in Ontario – the retail sales tax and local residential property taxes – are both clearly regressive.

FIGURE 7
Impact of Varying Shifting Assumptions
Corporate Tax – Federal and Provincial

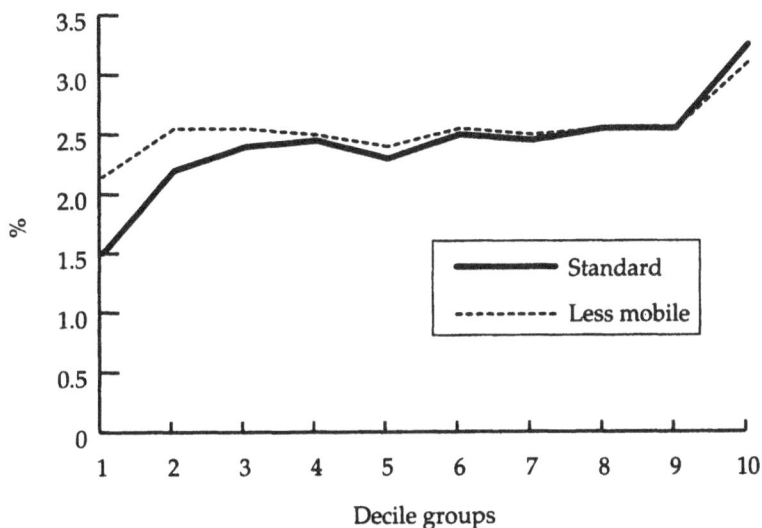

FIGURE 8
Impact of Varying Shifting Assumptions
Consumption Taxes – Federal and Provincial

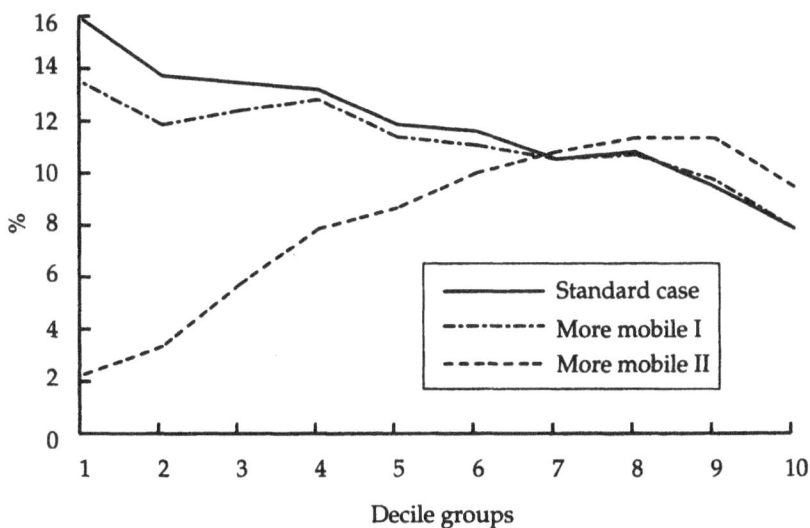

Finally, the results appear to be largely the same when we use alternative assumptions about shifting and tax incidence to conduct sensitivity analyses of our standard model.

Appendix 1: Aggregate Income and Taxes

Income, Ontario 1991	(millions of dollars)
Money Income	
Wages and salaries	143,127
Military pay and allowances	1,261
Net income of farm operators	593
Net income of non-farm operators excluding rent	10,304
Rental income	5,125
Other investment income	11,743
Mortgage income	1,502
Canadian dividends	339
Foreign investments	3,573
Life insurance	5,263
Foreign bond interest	3,573
Government employees pensions – federal	1,407
Government employees pensions – provincial	9
Private pension and annuity income	8,851
RRSP income	1,668
Federal family and youth allowances	259
World war pensions	305
War veterans allowance	174
Unemployment insurance benefits	5,251
Old age security payments	6,210
Scholar/research grants	269
Miscellaneous federal transfers	1,874
Child tax credit	664
GST credit	684
Ontario sales and property tax credit	421
Ontario direct relief	2,646
Old age/blind pensions	632
Workers' compensation benefits	1,880
Local relief	1,877
Canada pension plan income	5,921
Retained earnings	6,018
Capital gains on principal residences	−7419

Appendix 1 (continued)

Income, Ontario 1991	(millions of dollars)
Federal Taxes	
Federal income taxes	26,580
Employer/employee contributions to unemployment insurance	6,153
Employer/employee contributions to Canada Pension Plan	4,401
Direct taxes, from corporate and government business enterprises	3,873
GST	7,705
Customs import duties	2,003
Excise duties	1,020
Excise taxes	2,438
Air transportation tax	191
Provincial Taxes	
Income taxes	13,896
Employer health tax	2,652
Succession duties	2
Employer contributions to workers' compensation	2,443
Direct taxes, from corporate and government business enterprises	2,230
Amusement tax	151
Corporation tax (not on profits)	715
Gasoline tax	1,919
Motor vehicle licences and permits	202
Other licences, fees, and permits	95
Miscellaneous taxes on natural resources	30
Real property tax	115
Retail sales tax	8,707
Profits of liquor commissions	632
Lottery profits	459
Miscellaneous provincial indirect taxes	1,026
Local Taxes	
Licences, fees, and permits	200
Real and personal property taxes	10,749
Miscellaneous local taxes	2,193

Appendix 2: Variables Used for Shifting

Income component	SPSD variable
Wages and salaries	Earnings from employment
Military pay and allowances	Earnings from employment
Net income of farm operators	Farming net income
Net income of non-farm operators excluding rent	Self-employed income non-farming
Rental income	Equity of homeowners (market value– mortgage value)[a]
	Other investment income with net rental
Other investment income	Other investment income with net rental
Mortgage income	Other investment income with net rental
Canadian dividends	Canadian dividend income
Foreign investments	Other investment income with net rental
Life insurance income	Earnings from employment[b]
Foreign bond interest	Canadian dividend income
Government employees pensions – federal	Pension income
Government employees pensions – provincial	Pension income
Private pension and annuity income	Pension income
RRSP income	Canadian dividend income[c]
Federal family and youth allowances	Federal portion of family allowance
World war pensions	Pension income
War veterans allowance	Pension income
Unemployment insurance benefits	Unemployment insurance benefits
Old age security payments	Old age security benefits, guaranteed income supplement benefits, spouse's allowance
Scholar/research grants	Consumption of educational and cultural services
Miscellaneous federal transfers	Number of households[d]
Child tax credit	Child tax credit
GST credit	Federal sales tax credit
Ontario sales and property tax credit	Provincial tax credits
Ontario direct relief	Social assistance
Old age/blind pensions	Guaranteed income supplement provincial top-up
Workers' compensation benefits	Unemployment insurance benefits[e]
Local relief	Social assistance
Canada pension plan income	CPP payable
Retained earnings	Canadian dividend income
Capital gains on principal residences	Market value of homes

Appendix 2 (continued)

Income component	SPSD variable

Federal Taxes

Federal income taxes	Net federal income tax payable
Employer/employee contributions to unemployment insurance	Unemployment insurance contributions, Canadian dividend income, non-farming self-employed income
Employer/employee contributions to Canada Pension Plan	CPP contributions, Canadian dividend income, non-farming self-employed income
Direct taxes, from corporate and government business enterprises	Earnings from employment, other investment income with net rental, Canadian dividend income, interest income, income from equity in principal residence, total household expenditures, net federal income tax payable
GST	Federal retail sales tax
Customs import duties	Federal custom import duties
Excise duties	Household expenditures on alcoholic beverages, tobacco and gasoline, oil and grease
Excise taxes	Household expenditures on alcoholic beverages, tobacco and gasoline, oil and grease
Air transportation tax	Total household expenditures'

Provincial Taxes

Income taxes	Provincial income tax payable
Employer health tax	Employment income, Canadian dividend income, non-farming self-employed income
Succession duties	Employment income
Employer/employee contributions to workers' compensation	Employment income, Canadian dividend income, non-farming self-employed income
Direct taxes, from corporate and government business enterprises	Earnings from employment, other investment income with net rental, Canadian dividend income, interest income, income from equity, total household expenditures, net federal income tax payable
Amusement tax	Provincial amusement tax
Corporation tax (not on pofits)	Earnings from employment, other investment income with net rental, Canadian dividend income, interest income, income from equity in principal residence, total household expenditures, net federal income tax payable

Appendix 2 (continued)

Income component	SPSD variable
Gasoline tax	Consumption of gasoline, oil and grease, provincial industrial commodity tax payments
Motor vehicle licences and permits	Consumption of gasoline, oil and grease
Other licences, fees, and permits	Total household expenditures
Miscellaneous taxes on natural resouces	Total household expenditures[h]
Real property tax	Canadian dividend income[i]
Retail sales tax	Provincial retail sales tax payments, provincial industrial commodity tax payments
Profits of liquor commissions	Alcoholic beverage consumption
Lottery profits	Alcoholic beverage consumption[j]
Miscellaneous provincial indirect taxes	Total household expenditures

Local Taxes

Licences, fees, and permits	Total household expenditures[k]
Real and personal property taxes	Property tax payments, gross rent paid, other investment income with net rental, Canadian dividend income, total household expenditures, earnings from employment, income from equity in principal residence
Miscellaneous local taxes	Total household expenditure

Notes:

[a] This variable was constructed from Survey of Consumer Finances data. It is used to distribute the imputed value of owner-occupied housing.
[b] Life insuance ownership is assumed to be proportional to employment earnings.
[c] This variable is used as a proxy for the distribution of RRSP income.
[d] These transfers are distributed on a per capita basis.
[e] This variable is used as a proxy for the distribution of workers' compensation benefits.
[f] Air transportation tax payments are assumed to be proportional to total household expenditures.
[g] Small amounts of succession duty revenues are received from Ontario's succession duty tax that was abolished in 1971. Rather than distributing these duties on a per capita basis, employment income was used, as it is more closely correlated to wealth holdings.
[h] Taxes on natural resources are assumed to be shifted forward and embedded in a wide range of consumer products.
[i] The province collects a small amount of property taxes on commercial and industrial properties. These are distributed according to the receipt of dividend income.

ʲ The consumption of lottery tickets is assumed to be proportional to the consumption of alcoholic beverages.

ᵏ The burden of local licences, fees, and permits, which cover a wide range of services, is assumed to be proportional to household expenditures.

Appendix 3: Income Ranges by Decile Groups

Decile group 1	0 – 12,951
Decile group 2	12,951 – 20,076
Decile group 3	20,076 – 28,345
Decile group 4	28,345 – 35,839
Decile group 5	35,839 – 44,598
Decile group 6	44,598 – 53,104
Decile group 7	53,104 – 62,957
Decile group 8	62,957 – 76,425
Decile group 9	76,425 – 99,950
Decile group 10	99,950 +

Appendix 4: Tables

TABLE 1
Total Tax Incidence by Case (Deciles)

	1	2	3	4	5	6	7	8	9	10
Standard case	27.6	29.4	33.3	36.5	36.8	39.8	40.2	41.1	40.6	43.3
More mobile I	26	27.5	31.9	35.8	36.4	39.7	40.3	41.4	40.9	42.2
More mobile II	15.5	19.2	24.9	30.1	32.2	36.5	37.7	39	39.2	40.6
Less mobile	29.4	30.2	33.8	37	37.3	40.1	40.4	41.4	40.8	43.2

TABLE 2
Incidence by Level of Government – Standard Case (Deciles)

	1	2	3	4	5	6	7	8	9	10
Federal	10.6	12.4	15.6	18.5	19.1	21.3	21.7	22.4	22.3	23.1
Provincial	9.5	9.7	11.1	12.3	12.6	13.6	13.8	14.2	14	14.9
Local	7.4	7.2	6.6	5.7	5.1	4.8	4.7	4.5	4.3	5.3
Provincial & local	17	17	17.7	18	17.7	18.5	18.5	18.7	18.3	20.2

36 Sheila Block and Richard Shillington

TABLE 3
Progressivity of Selected Provincial Tax Bases (Deciles)

	1	2	3	4	5	6	7	8	9	10
Ontario personal income	0.2	1.2	2	3.1	3.9	4.9	5.2	5.6	6	7.3
Retail sales tax	5.3	4.5	4.4	4.3	3.8	3.6	3.5	3.5	3.1	2.7
Employer health tax	0.2	0.3	0.6	0.8	0.9	1	1.1	1.1	1.1	1.2
Ontario corpo- rate taxes	0.6	0.9	1	1	1	1.1	1.1	1.1	1.1	1.4
Residential property tax	4.4	3.9	3.5	2.8	2.6	2.3	2.3	2.2	2	2.2
Commercial & industrial property taxes	1.3	1.9	1.9	1.6	1.5	1.5	1.4	1.4	1.4	2.4

TABLE 4
Incidence Estimates by Family Type (Quintiles)

	1	2	3	4	5
Couples, one or more, elderly	37.2	32.1	33.3	34.4	35.5
Couples, no children	30.4	37.3	39.3	42.8	42.8
Couples, with children	31.6	34.5	40.6	42.2	43.2

TABLE 5
Impact of Varying Shifting and Assumptions (Deciles)

	1	2	3	4	5	6	7	8	9	10
Corporate Tax – Federal and Provincial										
Standard	1.5	2.2	2.4	2.4	2.3	2.5	2.5	2.6	2.6	3.3
Less mobile	2.1	2.6	2.6	2.5	2.4	2.6	2.6	2.6	2.6	3.1
Consumption Taxes – Federal and Provincial										
Standard case	15	12.9	12.7	12.5	11	10.4	9.8	9.8	8.6	6.9
More mobile I	12.6	11.2	11.6	11.8	10.6	10.2	9.8	9.8	8.8	7.2
More mobile II	2.3	3.3	5.5	7.6	8.1	9.4	9.8	10.2	9.9	8.1
Property Tax										
Standard total	5.7	5.8	5.4	4.5	4.1	3.8	3.7	3.6	3.4	4.6
Residential	4.4	3.9	3.5	2.8	2.6	2.6	2.3	2.2	2	2.2

TABLE 5 (continued)

	1	2	3	4	5	6	7	8	9	10
Commercial & industrial	1.3	1.9	1.9	1.6	1.5	1.5	1.4	1.4	1.4	2.4
More mobile I total	6.5	5.6	5.1	4.5	4.2	4.1	4	3.9	3.7	4
Residential	6.2	5	4.2	3.2	2.8	2.4	2.2	2.1	1.9	1.8
Commercial & industrial	0.3	0.6	1	1.3	1.4	1.7	1.7	1.8	1.8	2.2
Less mobile total	7.2	6.2	5.6	4.7	4.4	4	3.8	3.7	3.4	4.3
Residential	4.7	4	3.5	2.8	2.7	2.3	2.3	2.2	2	2.3
Commercial & industrial	2.4	2.2	2	1.9	1.7	1.7	1.6	1.5	1.4	2

Notes

* The authors would like to thank an informal advisory committee of Grant Cameron, W.I. Gillespie, Allan Maslove, and Michael Wolfson for their assistance.

1 The first proponents of lifetime income tax actually preceded the lifetime consumption theorists.
2 In addition to these considerations, data on income, expenditures, and taxes on a lifetime basis are inadequate.
3 This includes future consumption of goods and services, i.e., savings.
4 There is evidence, however, that at the upper end of the income distribution, after-tax income is the basis for negotiations on remuneration. To the extent that this is accurate, it would suggest that at upper-income levels, a portion of income tax may be shifted.
5 Critiques of Browning's assumptions are available in a number of sources. See, for example, Wolfson 1980, 123–6; Dahlby 1985, 137; and Davies 1992, 164, 179.
6 Ricardian equivalence suggests that changes in the relative amounts of tax and debt finance for a given level of public expenditures do not affect the level of real economic activity. See Barro 1974.
7 Refundable tax credits are not always considered transfers. In the National Accounts they are treated as a reduction in tax payable.
8 The marginal effective tax rate is a summary measure of the impact of corporate tax provisions on the profitability of investment projects. The effective tax rate is computed by calculating the amount of tax paid on profits earned on the last or marginal unit of capital held by the firm.

9 Mining is excluded because it has a different tax treatment. The mining capital stock has a very low weight in Ontario – around 4 per cent.
10 This analysis is based on Statistics Canada's Social Policy Simulation Database and Model. The assumptions and calculations underlying the results were prepared by the authors, and they are responsible for the use and interpretation of these data.
11 There are five units of analysis in SPSD/M: households, which are dependent on dwelling location; economic families, which include related persons living together as an economic unit within a single household; census families, which include a person, the person's spouse, if present, and any of their never-married children living in the economic family; the nuclear family, which is similar to the census family but excludes never-married children who are 18 or over; and individuals.
12 Twenty-five observations per quintile group in the family expenditure survey portion of the file was used as a cut-off for reporting results.
13 The quintile groups are based on the income distribution of the total population, not just the family types under consideration.

Bibliography

Ando, A., and Franco Modigliani. 1963. "The Life-Cycle Hypothesis of Saving: Aggregate Implementation and Tests." *American Economic Review* 53 (March): 55–84

Barro, Robert J. 1974. "Are Government Bonds Net Wealth?" *Journal of Political Economy* 82(6)

Bird, R.M., and N.E. Slack. 1978. *Residential Property Tax Relief in Ontario* Toronto: Ontario Economic Council

Browning, Edgar K. 1978. "The Burden of Taxation." *Journal of Political Economy* 8(4)(August): 649–71

Chen, Duanjie, and Jack Mintz. 1993. "Taxation of Capital in Ontario and Canada: An Interindustry and Interprovincial Comparison." In *Business Taxation in Ontario*, ed. Allan Maslove, 3–42. Toronto: University of Toronto Press

Dahlby, B.G. 1985. "The Incidence of Government Expenditures and Taxes in Canada: A Survey." In *Income Distribution and Economic Security in Canada*, ed. François Vaillancourt, 111–51. Toronto: University of Toronto Press

– 1993. "Payroll Taxes." In *Business Taxation in Ontario*, ed. Allan Maslove, 80–170. Toronto: University of Toronto Press

Davies, James B. 1992. "Tax Incidence: Annual and Lifetime Perspectives in the United States and Canada." In *Canada–U.S. Tax Comparisons*, eds John B. Shoven and John Whalley, 151–88. Chicago: University of Chicago Press

Davies J., F. St. Hilaire, and J. Whalley. 1984. "Some Calculations of Lifetime Tax Incidence." *American Economic Review* 74: 633–49

Dodge, D. 1975. "Impact of Tax, Transfer and Expenditure Policies of Government on the Distribution of Personal Incomes in Canada." *Review of Income and Wealth* 21: 1–52

Friedman, M. 1957. *A Theory of Consumption.* Princeton: Princeton University Press

Fullerton, Don, and Diane Lim Rogers. 1991. "Lifetime Versus Annual Perspectives on Tax Incidence." *National Tax Journal* 44(3): 278

Gillespie, W.I. 1980. *The Redistribution of Income in Canada.* Ottawa: Carleton University Press

Goffman, I.J. 1962. *The Burden of Canadian Taxation.* Toronto: Canadian Tax Foundation

Harberger, A.C. 1962. "The Incidence of the Corporate Income Tax." *Journal of Political Economy* 70: 215–40

Johnson, J.A. 1969. *The Incidence of Government Revenues and Expenditures.* A Study Prepared for The Ontario Committee on Taxation. Toronto: Queen's Printer

Kitchen, H.M. 1992. *Property Taxation in Canada.* Canadian Tax Foundation, Canadian Tax Paper No. 92

McKenzie, Kenneth J., and Jack M. Mintz. 1992. "Tax Effects on the Cost of Capital: A Canada–United States Comparison." In *Canada–U.S. Tax Comparisons,* eds J. Shoven and J. Whalley. Chicago: University of Chicago Press, 189–216

Maslove, A. *The Pattern of Taxation in Canada.* 1972. Study prepared for the Economic Council of Canada. Ottawa: Information Canada

Musgrave, Richard A. 1959. *The Theory of Public Finance.* New York: McGraw-Hill

Musgrave, R.A., P.B. Musgrave, and R. Bird. 1987. *Public Finance in Theory and Practice.* Toronto: McGraw-Hill Ryerson

Pechman, J.A., and B.A. Okner. 1974. *Who Bears the Tax Burden?* Washington: Brookings Institution

Ruggeri, G.C., and K.A. Bluck. 1992. "Treatment of Tax Transfers." *Public Finance Quarterly* 20(1)(January): 24–46

Ruggeri, G.C., D. Van Wart, and R. Howard. 1993. "The Redistributional Impact of Taxation in Canada. Mimeo

Vermaeten, Frank, W.I. Gillespie, and Arndt Vermaeten. Forthcoming. "Tax Incidence in Canada." *Canadian Tax Journal*

Whalley, J. 1984. "Innis Lecture: Regression or Progression: The Taxing Question of Incidence Analysis." *Canadian Journal of Economics* 17: 654–82

Wolfson, Michael C. 1980. "Tax Incidence in Canada: Robin Hood on Thin Ice." *Canadian Taxation* (Summer): 123–6

2 The Welfare Wall

An Analysis of the Welfare/Tax System in Ontario

KEN BATTLE and SHERRI TORJMAN

Introduction

The federal government made major changes to its personal, corporate, and consumption tax systems in the second half of the 1980s. In emulation of recent American tax reform, Canadian tax reform was founded on the twin precepts of broadening the tax base and reducing tax rates.

In his 1987 *White Paper on Tax Reform*, former federal finance minister Michael Wilson extolled lower tax rates "as the best way to reward success, by letting Canadians keep more of every dollar they earn to spend or save and invest as they see fit. Lower marginal tax rates also provide a continuing benefit to Canadians as their incomes grow in the future. This continuing benefit constitutes a general and potent incentive to engage in productive activity that will support economic growth, international competitiveness and job creation" (Wilson 1987, 4). While both the theory and practice of federal tax reform are open to considerable debate and doubt, the great store the government places on "rewarding success" and preventing the flight southward of highly paid Canadians in search of lower marginal tax rates reflects a firmly held conviction among orthodox economists and many upper-income people that high marginal tax rates are bad both for taxpayers and the economy.

At the same time as the federal government was pursuing its particular vision of fair taxation, a task force set up in 1986 by the Ontario government was carrying out an exhaustive review of the province's welfare system that culminated two years later in the landmark report

Transitions. While the federal and Ontario policy reviews diverged markedly both in subject matter and philosophy, there was in one respect a curious parallel between the two. Among its many findings and recommendations, the Ontario Social Assistance Review Committee (SARC) noted the long-recognized problem of astronomically high marginal tax rates imposed on welfare recipients who supplement their social assistance benefits with earnings from work. Not surprisingly, the potential exodus south of Ontario welfare recipients in search of lower marginal tax rates did not figure in the SARC report, but the work disincentive effects of uncoordinated tax and transfer programs that levy confiscatory rates of taxation on the poorest workers were identified as a major challenge for welfare reform.

The Social Assistance Review Committee cast its net very widely – more than one-quarter of its 274 recommendations dealt with programs and policies outside the welfare system proper – and acknowledged the need to include the tax system in its proposed reforms, but it did not undertake an analysis of the complex relationship between welfare, wages, and taxation. It proposed changes to ease the high welfare taxback on employment earnings and explored (though did not formally propose) the possibility of producing a "harmonized" system of income supplementation for the working poor, minimum wages, and social assistance. However, *Transitions* did not put forward any recommendations for changes to the tax system, instead calling upon the Ontario government "to adjust its tax system as necessary in order to maximize the incentives to work resulting from our specific recommendations" (Ontario Social Assistance Review Committee 1988, 297).

In 1991, Ontario established a Fair Tax Commission to study all aspects of taxation in the province. The Fair Tax Commission, in turn, commissioned the Caledon Institute of Social Policy to help unravel the complex relationship between the province's changing welfare system and the federal and provincial income tax systems, and to search out ways of easing the tax burden on the poor. The Caledon study grapples with the problem of the punitive tax burden imposed on welfare recipients who attempt to supplement their benefits by working in the paid labour force.

This paper summarizes the major findings of the study conducted for the Ontario Fair Tax Commission. It begins by reviewing salient aspects of the welfare/tax interface and actual and proposed changes to the Ontario welfare system. It then presents the major conclusions of our detailed, in-depth analysis of the tax burden on welfare recipients and our exploration of options for reform. More specifically, the paper:

1. describes Ontario's welfare system and those aspects that interact with the income tax system.
2. reviews recent and proposed reforms to Ontario's welfare system.
3. calculates the tax burden – defined here to include federal and provincial income taxes, payroll taxes, and reductions in social assistance and federal and provincial tax credits – on representative welfare households that supplement their income through wages. The study also discusses the additional costs of going to work for welfare recipients including the loss of in-kind benefits from welfare (e.g., supplementary health and dental care) and work-related expenses such as clothing, transportation, and child care.
4. explores a series of possible options for reform of the welfare, tax, and transfer systems and assesses the impact of these changes on the tax burden borne by households whose incomes combine wages and welfare.

The Welfare System

Welfare is the social program of last resort. Canadians may apply for welfare when they have no other source of income or when their needs exceed the resources available to them through employment, government benefits, or private sources.

Unlike other major programs of income support, welfare is the responsibility of provincial and territorial governments. However, the federal government shares in the costs of social assistance and social services on a 50-50 basis under the terms of the Canada Assistance Plan (CAP). CAP also spells out several conditions that must be met for receipt of federal funds: no work for welfare, appeal system, and no residence requirements. Moreover, various guidelines under CAP interpret what can and cannot be done under the Act.

While the 50-50 arrangement remains in theory, the federal government imposed a limit to its contributions to Ontario, Alberta, and British Columbia; from 1989–90 through 1994–5, federal transfers under CAP to these three provinces – which together account for 61 per cent of all welfare recipients in Canada – are limited to a five per cent annual increase. The "cap on CAP" has had a severe impact on Ontario, in particular, because of its high unemployment and escalating welfare rolls during the recession of the early 1990s. The province has had to contribute much more than its 50 per cent share to cover the costs of social assistance and social services. In fact, the federal government's share of eligible social assistance costs fell to 28 per cent in 1992–3.

All provinces and territories have developed extensive and complex regulations and policies that govern their respective welfare systems. Each jurisdiction has its own rules regarding eligibility, benefit levels, exemptions on earned income, monitoring and enforcement, and appeals. The rules also vary with respect to the eligibility of Aboriginal persons, who may qualify for provincial welfare if they live off reserve. Despite the differences among jurisdictions, all welfare systems have several features in common.

Some of the general elements of welfare are described here in order to identify those features that have direct and/or indirect relevance to the tax system. They include: liquid asset exemptions, needs tests, rates of assistance, and earnings exemptions.

Liquid Asset Exemptions

"Liquid asset exemptions" refer to the amount of cash or cash-convertible assets that a given household may have and still be eligible for welfare assistance. While these levels vary by province and territory, they cannot exceed the guidelines set by the federal government. The maximum federal levels, last set in July 1980, are:

- $2,500 for single persons and $3,000 for persons who are aged or disabled;
- $5,000 for persons with one dependent (spouse or child) and $5,500 when applicants or spouses are aged or disabled;
- an extra $500 for the second and each additional dependent;
- an additional amount where this has been placed in a special fund or trust for purposes that the province considers to be socially important – such as the education of a child or the purchase of a piece of equipment to overcome a disabling condition.

In Ontario, the liquid asset exemptions in 1992 for unemployable applicants were $2,500 for single persons, $5,000 for single parents with one dependent, and $3,000 for single persons with disabilities. For applicants considered to be employable, municipal welfare administrators determine the allowable level of liquid assets. For single persons, assets equal to one to two weeks' assistance may be exempted (one to three months' assistance in the case of temporarily unemployable persons). Families may have assets equal to one to three months' assistance. Maximum exemptions ($2,500 for single persons and $5,000 for couples plus $500 per dependent) may apply to households to be transferred to Family Benefits.

The liquid asset guidelines can affect the tax treatment of welfare recipients. The fact that welfare households are restricted in the amount of liquid assets means that there are limits to the interest payments that they may receive from bank savings or bonds. An increase in liquid assets could translate into higher interest income, which, in turn, would generate a higher tax burden for welfare recipients. The additional tax burden could potentially offset any benefits that might accrue through more generous asset guidelines.

Needs Testing

The central eligibility criterion for all welfare systems throughout the country is the needs test. A needs test takes into account households' basic needs such as food, clothing, shelter, and utilities. It also considers households' special needs such as medication, health-related diets, or equipment for a disabling condition.

The needs test identifies the household's resources available to meet those needs. Resources include earnings, government benefits, private savings, support payments, insurance claims, pensions, and income derived from any other source. Certain government transfers, such as the refundable Goods and Services Tax (GST) credit, are considered exempt by most jurisdictions in the determination of welfare eligibility. Some provinces include government benefits as income for the purpose of establishing initial eligibility for welfare. These benefits are not counted as income, however, in setting the actual levels of assistance.

Households *may* be eligible for welfare assistance if their needs exceed the available resources as determined by the needs test. We emphasize the word "may" because applicants still must meet provincial definitions and the liquid asset exemption guidelines.

The needs test is relevant to the tax system for the following reason. Low-income households are eligible for several refundable tax credits including the federal child tax benefit and GST credit and the Ontario sales tax and property tax credits. If these credits were counted as income in the initial determination of welfare assistance, they could have the effect of disqualifying many households because the credits could reduce the budget deficit to the point where households would be deemed not to qualify for assistance. Thus a positive initiative intended to help low-income families could inadvertently have a neg-ative impact from a welfare perspective, effectively denying the new benefit to the poorest of the poor. This is not a hypothetical problem. It arose when the federal government brought in the refundable child tax credit in 1978 and the refundable sales tax credit in 1986; some municipalities in Manitoba, for example, initially counted the sales tax credit as income for welfare purposes and had to be pressured to reverse this punitive policy.

Another problem related to the welfare/tax credit relationship is more insidious because it is unwritten, usually not publicly acknowledged, and virtually impossible to document. There is no statutory indexation of welfare benefits in any jurisdiction in Canada (except for the Financial Support Program in Quebec for persons with severe disabilities). Instead, provincial governments adjust their welfare rates in an ad hoc fashion. Informally, some provincial officials have acknowledged that increases to tax credits generally are taken into account when welfare rates are set. This means that an increase in the value of tax credits may be offset by a corresponding decrease (from inflation) in the value of welfare benefits.

Rates of Assistance

Each province and territory employs a unique set of rules to determine its rates of social assistance. Rates vary on the basis of several factors including family size, age of children, marital status of the family head, employability of the head, and other characteristics such as the presence of a disabling condition.

The level of welfare assistance has clear and obvious implications for work incentives and the after-tax status of welfare poor and working poor households. Most jurisdictions, Ontario included, provide substantially lower welfare benefits to recipients deemed to be employable. The rates of welfare assistance for Ontario are outlined in the discussion of the Caledon Tax/Transfer Model.

Earnings Exemptions

"Earnings exemption guidelines" refer to the amount of income that welfare recipients may earn from outside employment without affecting their welfare entitlement. Once their earnings exceed the specified limit, their welfare cheques are reduced by a designated amount.

These guidelines vary widely by province and territory. In some provinces, such as Quebec, earnings exemptions take the form of a flat-rate amount. Welfare cheques are reduced by one dollar for every

dollar of income earned over and above that amount. In other jurisdictions, such as Alberta, exemptions are expressed as a percentage of
earnings. Recipients may keep up to a certain percentage of their
employment-related earnings (to a designated maximum) before their
welfare cheques are reduced. Still other provinces, such as Ontario,
use a combination of flat-rate and variable exemptions whereby recipients may earn up to a specified amount with no reduction to their
welfare benefits, as well as an additional amount that represents a set
percentage of their earnings (above which welfare is reduced). For
example, single employable recipients of General Welfare Assistance
in Ontario can earn up to $75 a month with no offset to their welfare
and can keep an additional 25 cents for every dollar earned above this
level.

Welfare Reform in Ontario

Social Assistance Review Committee

In July 1986, the Ministry of Community and Social Services announced the appointment of the Social Assistance Review Committee
(SARC) to undertake a comprehensive examination of social assistance
and related services in Ontario. The review of the welfare system had
been long overdue. Both the General Welfare Assistance Act and the
Family Benefits Act, which form the legislative base of Ontario's welfare system, had not been changed since they came into effect in 1959
and 1967, respectively.

Because the welfare system in Ontario is governed by two separate
acts, it is called a two-tier system. "Two-tier" refers to the fact that two
different levels of government are responsible for delivering welfare
assistance. Under the General Welfare Assistance Act, municipalities
have primary responsibility for welfare recipients considered to be
employable. The provincial government assumes responsibility under
the Family Benefits Act for recipients likely to be unemployed over an
extended period of time.

After an extensive study of the welfare system and public consultations, the Social Assistance Review Committee presented its findings
in the *Transitions* report issued in 1988. Before presenting any proposals
for reform, *Transitions* set out the principles upon which reform should
be based: eligibility (the right to assistance), adequacy, accessibility,
personal development, personal responsibility, individual rights,

respect for family life, respect for diversity, accountability of the system, and shared responsibility.

Transitions addressed four key issues: 1) the urgent need to simplify and improve Ontario's welfare system; 2) the development of means to help recipients with employment potential move off welfare and into the labour market; 3) the need for a more adequate and equitable system of income security not only in Ontario but throughout the entire country as well; and 4) the importance of providing adequate supports to sustain and promote the health and well-being of low-income individuals and families.

In addition to improving the adequacy of the system for current recipients, SARC believed that it was equally important to encourage employable recipients to enter or move back into the labour market. It proposed a series of changes intended to reduce the work disincentives in the existing system.

Transitions suggested that a clear policy be developed regarding the exemptions on earned income. It also recommended that welfare recipients be allowed to keep more of their employment earnings. This measure not only would reward work-related efforts, but also would help recognize work-related costs. In addition, social assistance calculations for the purpose of determining monthly assistance payments should be based on net income rather than gross income.

In order to promote the employability of recipients considered able to work, SARC proposed the introduction of a new staff function called "opportunity planning." This function would be separate from that of welfare workers concerned primarily with the determination of benefits. Opportunity planners would help recipients assess their employment skills, provide them with relevant training and job-related information, and help them develop an individual action plan that would identify specific work goals.

SARC also recommended several related reforms to ease the transition between welfare and the paid labour force. It proposed that the Work Incentive (WIN) program be enhanced by allowing former welfare recipients to maintain, for a certain period, their access to income-in-kind such as prescription drugs. WIN also was seen as the basis for a new income supplementation scheme.

In May 1989, the Ontario government responded to *Transitions* by announcing a package of reforms worth $415 million. These initiatives represented immediate measures that could be taken as part of the first stage of welfare reform proposed by SARC. Effective January 1990, rates of assistance were increased by six per cent. The province instituted a more adequate method for calculating shelter allowances by introducing a base allowance that reflects more accurately the cost of housing as well as a variable component that supplements actual shelter costs up to a designated maximum.

The age categories for benefits for children of welfare recipients were reduced from three to two – one for children up to age 12 and the other for children ages 13 and older. Payments for children under General Welfare Assistance were increased to the levels under Family Benefits. Back-to-school and winter clothing allowances for children, which formerly applied only to households on Family Benefits, were made mandatory for families on General Welfare Assistance as well.

In October 1989, the Ontario government also introduced the Supports to Employment Program (STEP). STEP is a package of regulatory changes that affect the way in which the province treats the earned income of welfare recipients. Its purpose is to ensure that welfare recipients are better off financially by taking employment or training opportunities and increasingly are better off with each additional dollar earned. Other regulatory changes were introduced in October 1991; the following description covers both the initial and the subsequent revisions.

Under STEP, earnings are calculated on the basis of net rather than gross income. Prior to the change, Ontario was the only province aside from Manitoba and (for long-term recipients) Nova Scotia that calculated earnings exemptions on the basis of gross income. Payroll deductions for Canada Pension Plan contributions, unemployment insurance premiums, union dues, contributions to registered pension plans, and income taxes are subtracted from gross earnings.

The earnings exemption in Ontario consists of a flat-rate (a lump-sum amount) and a variable component (a designated percentage of earnings). In addition to allowing full payroll deductions, STEP increased both the flat-rate and variable components of the earnings and training exemption. For example, the flat-rate component increased from $50 to $75 for single persons on General Welfare Assistance and from $160 to $175 for single-parent families. The variable exemption was introduced at 20 per cent in 1989 and then increased to 25 per cent as of 1 October 1991. These increases were intended to reflect more accurately the costs of going to work and to encourage welfare recipients to move into paid employment. The earnings/training exemptions for various households are outlined in table 1. The first

TABLE 1
Earnings/Training/Exemptions, GWA and FBA, 1992

	GWA			FBA	
Single person	Two-adult family	Single parent	Single disabled	Single parent	Disabled family
$75 + 25% of net earnings/ training over $75	$150 + 25% of net earnings/ training over $150	$175 + 25% of net earnings/ training over $175	$160 + 25% of net earnings/ training over $160	$175 + 25% of net earnings/ training over $175	$185 + 25% of net earnings/ training over $185

three columns refer to General Welfare Assistance (GWA) and the fourth to the sixth columns to Family Benefits (FBA).

STEP also permits the deduction of child care costs from net earnings or net training allowances before calculating monthly welfare assistance. For unlicensed child care, up to $390 a month may be deducted for children 5 years of age and under and $346 a month for children between the ages of 6 and 12. In special circumstances, the deduction may be allowed for children over age 12. Families using licensed child care, by contrast, may deduct actual costs.

For both licensed and unlicensed care, a payment may be made to cover the first month's cost of child care. This payment is intended to assist families with cash flow problems that they may face when returning to work.

An Employment Start-Up Benefit and an Employment Start-Up Allowance of up to $250 in any 12-month period is provided through Family Benefits and General Welfare Assistance, respectively. These benefits are intended to assist individuals with initial expenses related to work or training.

Recipients who no longer qualify for welfare because their incomes are slightly higher than their needs as determined by the needs test still may retain eligibility for supplementary health benefits, such as subsidized prescription drugs. A "buffer zone" of up to $50 for single persons and $100 for families was introduced to allow households that miss the financial test of eligibility by these amounts to continue to qualify for health-related benefits. Prior to this measure, the loss of eligibility for welfare assistance meant the loss of health benefits as well. Finally, the "120-hour rule," which made single parents ineligible for Family Benefits if they worked more than 120 hours per month, was withdrawn.

As part of its efforts to reduce welfare spending, which skyrocketed because of the recession, the Ontario government announced that, as of August 1992, the STEP program no longer would permit the deduction of relevant earnings exemptions for the initial establishment of eligibility. This action has had the effect of raising the income threshold upon which the determination of eligibility is made, thereby reducing the numbers of households that potentially may qualify under the program. For those that still qualify, the flat-rate and variable components of the exemption may not be deducted from earnings until after three months. This regulatory change has had the effect of virtually excluding working poor Ontarians for qualifying for some welfare assistance. They now must reduce their earnings to become eligible for welfare – a strong disincentive to employment.

As a further cost-cutting measure, the province announced that, effective 1 August 1993, it would reduce the flat-rate component of the earnings exemption for certain households. It lowered the flat-rate component of the exemption for single employable persons and for families on GWA from $75 to $50 a month and from $150 to $100 a month, respectively. It also reduced the flat-rate component of the earnings exemption for single-parent families on FBA from $175 to $120 a month.

Advisory Group on New Social Assistance Legislation

In May 1990, the Ontario government created a 12-member Advisory Group on New Social Assistance Legislation. Its mandate was to advise the minister of Community and Social Services on how to transform the recommendations in *Transitions* into new social assistance legislation. While the minister seemed anxious to proceed with reform, the government did not appear to be similarly committed.

When the NDP government took office in September 1990, it reactivated the Advisory Group and requested that it explore ways to speed up the process of reform. The deliberations of the Advisory Group were informed by the work of six Project Teams, which examined legal issues, disability determination, benefit structure, employment services, welfare to First Nations communities, delivery, and funding.

In March 1991, the Advisory Group presented a report on short-term reform of the welfare system. Entitled *Back on Track*, the report put forward 88 actions that the Ontario government could take in the short term to address many of the problems that *Transitions* had identified in relation to the inadequacy of benefits, complexities, and unfairness inherent in the welfare system.

The actions put forward in the document were intended to improve benefits, ease access to and movement off welfare, improve accountability, provide incentives to work, and improve the funding of the welfare system. These were considered to be short-term actions because they could be taken without new legislation. In response to the proposals in *Back on Track*, the province announced in its April 1991 budget an additional $215 million for welfare reform. While almost two-thirds of the recommendations in the *Back on Track* report were implemented, one of the most significant changes was the expansion of the STEP program, earlier described.

After the release of *Back on Track*, the Advisory Group directed its attention toward its original mandate – the preparation of a report on a unified social assistance act. The similarities and differences in the two acts governing General Welfare Assistance and Family Benefits were identified. The issues raised in the *Transitions* report that related to the integration of the programs also were considered. A total of 240 items were identified. The six Project Teams addressed the issues relevant to their respective mandates, prepared background papers, and developed options for presentation to the Advisory Group.

In June 1992, the Advisory Group issued its report, *Time for Action: Towards a New Social Assistance System for Ontario*. The report concluded that the Ontario welfare system must be redesigned because it is simply too complex and costly to continue without fundamental reform. Anything less than a comprehensive overhaul would represent only minor changes to a system that is basically unsound.

One of the fundamental tenets of reform is that social assistance must return to its original purpose of being a last-resort line of defence for persons in need of financial assistance rather than the first line of defence against economic adversity. The welfare system must be made more active in terms of supporting the movement of recipients into the mainstream of society and linking them with education, housing, child care, counselling, and training programs.

Time for Action set out 52 recommendations for reforming and developing a social assistance system that is supportive rather than punitive. Specific recommendations called for legislation that would result in a system based on need only, with two categories of recipient: persons with disabilities and others. Welfare should be delivered through a unified system with a single-tier delivery structure and provincial responsibility for full funding in order to ensure greater fairness and equitable treatment. Social assistance rates should be based on a market basket of goods that would be updated annually to provide an adequate standard of living. Specific criteria for decision-making should be identified to help reduce the discretion. Opportunity planning should be an integral aspect of the welfare system.

"Turning Point"

In July 1993, the Ontario government released the report *Turning Point*, which announced its intention to dismantle the welfare system and replace it with two new income programs: the Ontario Child Income Program and the Ontario Adult Benefit. In order to help adults make the transition to independence, an employment planning system – JOB LINK – would connect them to training, education, and jobs. While the report provided no specific details on program design and delivery features, it did lay out the general philosophy and framework of reform.

In order better to deal with child poverty and to treat all low-income families equitably, children would be removed entirely from the welfare system and served by a new income-tested program available to both welfare and working-poor families. In place of the child-based portion of social assistance that currently goes to welfare households, all families with children that qualify on the basis of their net incomes would receive benefits under the Ontario Child Income Program. Eligibility and benefits would be determined through an assessment of the income tax returns filed each year by families at tax time, as is the case with the federal child tax benefit.

In addition to financial assistance designed exclusively for children, the province would introduce a benefit intended only for adults. The Ontario Adult Benefit would be delivered as a single cash payment that would replace existing welfare payments under General Welfare Assistance and Family Benefits.

Eligibility for the Ontario Adult Benefit would be determined on the basis of applicants' income and resources. The benefit would take into account the cost of food, clothing, shelter, and personal needs. Its level would be set in relation to the provincial minimum wage. This would help ensure that Ontarians are always better off working, because benefits never will be a more attractive alternative than paid employment. Moreover, people who are able to work and who are actively engaged in employment planning, job search, or training activities would receive a special allowance.

Additional financial assistance would be provided to persons with disabilities to help them live independently and find training or work opportunities. There would be no separate category of assistance for persons with disabilities based on arbitrary assumptions about the people who are classified in that category. The level of financial aid paid to recipients with disabilities would be determined by individual need. Many items currently provided at the discretion of municipalities would be made mandatory. A long-term supplement would be made available under the program for low-income persons who are 60 years or older and to persons who cannot reasonably be expected to work on a full-time basis.

A new program – JOB LINK – would be introduced to help recipients of the Ontario Adult Benefit prepare for and find employment. JOB LINK would consist of five major elements: employability assessment; employment planning; education, training or employment preparation, and placement; support services; and monitoring and review.

Ontario has yet to decide what role the municipalities would play, if any, in the delivery of the new Ontario Adult Benefit. As far as funding the new program is concerned, the province is committed to assuming 100 per cent of the cost of financing social assistance. However, this change would require the municipalities to take on some offsetting responsibilities in other areas of government services, since the goal is to keep the respective provincial and municipal shares of financing the same.

The Caledon Tax/Transfer Model

General Description

The Caledon Tax/Transfer Model was used to analyse the interaction between the welfare and tax/transfer systems. The model can simulate the impact of a number of factors – such as changes to earnings, income mixes, earnings exemptions, tax rates, tax credits, thresholds, and reduction rates – for any given household. In short, the model simulates how the tax and transfer systems (including welfare) currently work and how they might operate if one or several parameters were changed. It was used here to estimate the interactive effects of income taxes and transfers on the earnings of welfare recipients.

The limitations of the Caledon Tax/Transfer Model lie in the fact that it does not include survey or administrative data; it is a simulation model only, not a model directly grounded in one or more sets of data. It is not possible, for example, to determine from the Caledon Model how many households would "win" or "lose" from different tax/transfer changes. Nor is it possible to estimate the costs of these changes. In order to answer questions with respect to winners and losers as well as potential costs for different options, it is necessary to use a model based on survey and/or administrative data. To our knowledge, no such model exists that adequately could serve the purposes of our study for the Ontario Fair Tax Commission, so we chose instead to do the job ourselves using our own simulation model tailored to the task at hand.

In our analysis of the tax/transfer systems, we not only explored the traditional meaning of taxes – i.e., federal and provincial income taxes – but also expanded the concept to include both direct taxes and indirect taxes. "Direct taxes" refer to payroll taxes, federal and Ontario income taxes, and the welfare taxback. "Indirect taxes" refer to the drop in the value of refundable tax credits with increased earnings.

While the model counts as income the federal GST credit and child tax benefit as well as Ontario property and sales tax credits delivered through the tax system, it does not measure the tax burden that welfare recipients bear through the payment of property and sales taxes or the GST. Our study looks only at federal and Ontario income taxes and federal payroll taxes, not the full range of taxes imposed by the three levels of government. We do not attempt to quantify the loss of in-kind benefits, such as subsidized housing and supplementary health and dental benefits. Nor do we estimate employment-related costs such as transportation and clothing; our model can include child care expenses, but (as explained below) we assumed for the purposes of this study that these were fully subsidized.

The Caledon Tax/Transfer Model as configured for this study integrates the key elements of the federal/Ontario income tax system and the Ontario welfare system. Our study is built on the assumption that full welfare income is the baseline that serves as the standard for various points of comparison, above all the measurement of our expanded concept of tax burden.

The model shows what happens to disposable income (i.e., total earnings from welfare, work, child benefits, and federal and provincial refundable tax credits, minus payroll taxes and federal and provincial income taxes) of welfare recipients as they move into the labour market and as their earnings from paid employment increase. It also gauges the costs of employment by measuring the total taxes that welfare recipients pay with increased earnings. As noted earlier, taxes include not only compulsory payroll deductions and federal and provincial income taxes, but also the loss in the value of income-tested tax credits (i.e., the child tax benefit, the GST credit, and the Ontario property and sales tax credits) and in social assistance as earnings rise. A key measure of the cost of going to work used in our study is the marginal tax rate, which in essence expresses the total tax burden as a percentage of the increase in income for each ascending employment earnings level (we used $1,000 annual earnings increments, which amounts to $83.33 a month).

Assumptions

In developing the model for this project, several assumptions had to be made with respect to household type, sources of income, base year, tax credits, welfare assistance, child care expenses, and low-income measures. These assumptions are described below.

Household Type

This paper presents the results of the welfare/tax interface for two representative households: single employable persons and single-parent families with one child, age 2. However, our full study for the Ontario Fair Tax Commission looked at 11 household types: single employable persons; single persons with disabilities; single-parent families with one child age 2, two children ages 3 and 5, and two children ages 10 and 15; one-earner couples with one child age 2, two children ages 3 and 5, and two children ages 10 and 15; and two-earner couples with one child age 2, two children ages 3 and 5, and two children ages 10 and 15.

This combination of households was chosen for several reasons. We wanted to ensure that the analysis would include both General Welfare Assistance recipients (i.e., single unemployed persons and two-parent families) and Family Benefits recipients (single persons with disabilities and single-parent families). We also wanted to explore the weight of the tax burden incurred by households of different sizes and with varying combinations of younger and other children, since the federal child tax benefit, the GST credit, and welfare all vary their payments according to children's ages.

Sources of Income

The households used in the model were assumed to derive income from three major sources: employment earnings, social assistance, and government transfers (i.e., the federal child tax benefit and the GST credit, and Ontario property and sales tax credits). We assumed that the households had no income from other sources such as investments, alimony, maintenance payments, workers' compensation, Canada Pension Plan disability benefits, or private insurance.

Base Year

The year 1992 was selected as the base year for the assumptions and calculations used in this model. With respect to welfare incomes, in particular, the rates reflect the social assistance that was paid in the second half of 1992 in order to include the three per cent increase to shelter allowances that took effect 1 July 1992.

Tax Credits

Because of their differing payment schedules, a decision had to be made regarding the value of the federal and provincial refundable tax credits. There were two options from which to choose. The first approach was to use the 1991 value of the credits in order to reflect the actual amounts that households would have received in 1992, since there is a delay of varying lengths between the time that the various credits are applied for (through the income tax form) and the time they are paid. The second possibility was to use the 1992 value of the credits in order to reflect the interaction of the tax and transfer systems in that year. We selected the latter approach because we felt it was more relevant to the task at hand – i.e., to analyse the interaction of the tax and transfers systems. Moreover, we wanted to ensure that the amounts used in the model were as up to date as possible.

Child Tax Benefit A key issue that had to be resolved was the value of the child benefits to employ in the model. While 1992 was selected as the base year, the federal child tax benefit came into effect as of 1 January 1993. Nonetheless, it would have been inappropriate to build in the former system of child benefits when it would be obsolete in only a few months.

We therefore decided to incorporate the new child tax benefit into the model as though it had actually been introduced in 1992. We used the 1993 value of the benefit and its family income threshold because, in fact, they would have been the same had the new scheme been launched in 1992: inflation was only 2.3 per cent in 1992, which is below Ottawa's 3 per cent partial indexation trigger.

The basic child tax benefit is $1,020 and there is a $213 supplement for each child age 6 and younger for whom child care receipts are not available. In addition to the basic child tax benefit, working poor families are eligible for an earned-income supplement of up to $500 per family per year. Families with net incomes of up to $25,921 receive the maximum child tax benefit, which phases out at a rate of 2.5 per cent for families with one child and 5 per cent for families with more than one child. The earned-income supplement phases in at a rate of 8 per cent of employment earnings over $3,750 and phases out at 10 per cent on net family income over $20,921; the maximum $500 goes to families in roughly the $10,000 to $21,000 earnings range.

GST Credit The GST credit incorporated in the model represents the actual value of the credit for 1992. The annual maximum amounts of $199 per adult and $105 per child were payable to all households with net incomes up to $25,921. The credit is reduced by five per cent of net family income above the $25,921 threshold. The first child in single-parent families receives the adult amount.

In addition to the basic GST credit, a GST supplement is provided to single adults and single parents with net incomes over $6,456. The supplement phases in above $6,456 at the rate of two per cent and reaches its maximum amount of $105 once net income reaches $11,706. The supplement remains at this level until net family income of $25,921, above which it phases out at a rate of five per cent, disappearing once net family income hits $28,021.

Ontario Tax Credits Ontario tax credits were calculated on the basis of their value in 1992. The sales tax credit was worth $100 per adult and $50 per child. Ontario property tax credits were calculated by using as occupancy cost the maximum shelter allowance (including maximum subsidy) that the household received as the housing component of its welfare benefit.

Welfare Assistance

The calculations employed for this model represent the value of welfare benefits under the General Welfare Assistance and Family Benefits programs as of 1 July 1992. These rates were used because Ontario introduced a three per cent increase to the shelter component of its welfare benefits on that date. The earnings exemptions are based on their value in the STEP program as of 1 January 1992.

Welfare recipients' gross monthly employment earnings were taken as the base upon which to calculate welfare income. Deductions from gross monthly earnings were made for Canada Pension Plan contributions and unemployment insurance premiums and for federal and Ontario income taxes. The remaining amount represents net employment earnings. For the purposes of this analysis, it was assumed that welfare recipients made no contributions in respect of union dues or registered pension plans and RRSPs, even though these contributions are permitted under STEP in determining net employment earnings; few low-wage earners belong to unions or registered pension plans or contribute to RRSPs.

Two additional amounts were then deducted from net employment earnings: the flat-rate and variable exemptions allowed by STEP. The flat-rate exemption is a specified amount that is deducted from net earnings. The value of this exemption varies by family size. The flat-rate exemptions employed in the calculations were $75 for single employable persons and $175 for single-parent families.

The variable exemption represents an amount that is deducted from net earnings over and above the flat-rate exemption. The variable exemption for all households was 25 per cent of net earnings over the designated flat-rate exemption.

The earnings that remain after the flat-rate and variable exemptions are deducted from net employment earnings represent the "welfare taxback." This is the amount by which households' welfare cheques are reduced in respect of their employment earnings. The welfare taxback is deducted from maximum welfare entitlement to determine the actual welfare received by household.

Welfare entitlement consists of two components. The first component is the maximum amount of basic assistance to which households are entitled if they have no employment earnings. The second component is the maximum shelter allowance, which consists of a basic and a variable shelter allowance.

The households for which results are presented here were eligible for the following monthly maximum basic allowances and shelter allowances: $246 and $410 for single employable persons, and $563 and $645 for single-parent families with one child. No additional amounts were included for items of special assistance aside from the winter clothing allowance and the back-to-school allowance provided automatically to all families with children. In 1992, the winter clothing allowance was $104 per child for recipients of General Welfare Assistance and Family Benefits. Similarly, all families received a lump-sum back-to-school benefit of $68 for children between the ages of 4 and 12 and $125 for children ages 13 and over.

Child Care Expenses

The current STEP rules allow families to deduct up to $390 a month for children 5 years of age and under and up to $346 a month for children between the ages of 6 and 12 for unlicensed care. Recipients may deduct the actual amounts paid for licensed care.

For this application of the Caledon Model, we had to make assumptions as to whether households with children were using licensed or unlicensed care and the amounts they were deemed to pay. Our first option was to assume the availability of licensed care. The second possibility was to assume that recipients use unlicensed care and to incorporate the maximum amount of the deduction in the STEP deductions. The fully licensed care scenario, in which recipients pay nothing, and the unlicensed care scenario, in which recipients pay full maximum amounts, represent the two ends of the continuum of child care costs.

The difficulty in deciding whether to employ figures that represent licensed or unlicensed child care arises from the fact that families often use varying combinations of care. Their child care arrangements do not fit any "pure" model. Many families combine licensed arrangements such as a day care facility, preschool program, nursery, or kindergarten with various forms of unlicensed care provided by a spouse or other relative, neighbour, friend, or nanny.

One way to resolve this problem is to employ actual average child care costs in the STEP calculations. Under Family Benefits, families with one child, two children, and three or more children paid average child care costs of $212, $262, and $274, respectively, in June 1992. Under General Welfare Assistance, families with one child, two children, and three or more children paid an average of $262, $324, and $353, respectively, for child care in that month.

While actual averages reflect real costs, several problems arise in using these figures. Because these averages represent the amounts paid by all families, they combine the expenditure for young children under age 6 as well as other children between the ages of 7 and 12. In addition, the actual amount paid by some families may be underrepresented because the figures include the very low fees (e.g., $1 or $2 a day) paid by some families that qualify for subsidized child care. In some cases, families may pay nothing at all, thereby lowering the overall average costs. The net result is that actual averages likely underrepresent the real amounts that families with very young children pay for child care. This is a problem in that we wanted the model to reflect, the greatest extent possible, the cost burden borne by families with very young children – i.e., the true cost of going to work.

Moreover, actual averages do not reflect the fact that welfare households re-entering or entering the labour market for the first time work varying numbers of hours. Some families may work only several hours a week, while others may work several hours a day for the entire week. Actual averages make no distinction in the costs incurred by families that work only a few hours a week as opposed to families that derive much or even most of their income from paid employment.

In short, each of the choices with respect to child care costs has its own associated problems in representing the "real world." The assumption of fully licensed child care at no cost to recipients clearly underrepresents the expenditure for many families that do not have access to subsidized care. On the other hand, the selection of the maximum cost scenario is not a true reflection of reality in that it excludes recipients who receive full subsidy for licensed care or whose children may be in kindergarten in the public school system. Moreover, if the full costs of such care are deducted from the STEP formula, then the disposable income derived through our calculations likely would come out much higher than is actually the case for most families. Finally, the use of actual averages reflects so many diverse factors that the numbers themselves are almost meaningless in terms of what any given family actually may pay.

We decided to assume that welfare recipients who were trying to return to work were receiving fully subsidized child care and were not paying any fees. We therefore ran the model using zero for child care costs. In effect, we wanted to establish a "clean" baseline of interaction without the complications that arise as a result of highly variable child care arrangements that, in any case, are not central to the focus of this study.

Low-Income Measures

This study used Statistics Canada's after-tax low-income cut-offs with which to compare the federal and Ontario income tax thresholds as well as the income levels where eligibility for welfare benefits ceases. We estimated the 1992 after-tax low-income cut-offs for a metropolitan area (500,000 or more) to be $12,867 for single persons, $17,447 for families of two, and $26,567 for families with four members. When using poverty lines, we always employed the concept of after-tax income, defined as total income (from welfare, paid work, the child tax benefit, and federal and Ontario refundable tax credits) minus federal and Ontario income taxes.

Key Findings

Single Employable Persons

Marginal Tax Rate (Figure 1)

The marginal tax rate for single employable welfare recipients illustrates the classic "welfare trap": very high marginal tax rates at very low levels of earnings. The marginal tax rate begins at 75 per cent for the first $1,000 of employment earnings (which means that recipients keep only one-quarter of what they earn), rises to 86 per cent at $7,000 (the earnings level at which federal income tax begins), and hits a peak of 87 per cent at $9,000 (the earnings level at which Ontario income tax begins). The marginal tax rate declines slightly to 84 per cent at $10,000 to $12,000 and 83 per cent at $13,000.

The marginal tax rate then plummets to 33 per cent at work earnings of $14,000 and remains flat until $24,000. The steep decline can be attributed to the fact that single employable persons with earnings of $14,000 are no longer eligible for welfare and therefore no longer pay a welfare taxback. *The welfare taxback is the major reason for the astronomical marginal tax rates facing welfare recipients, dwarfing all other elements of their total tax burden including federal and Ontario income taxes, payroll taxes, and the decline in refundable tax credits.*

Federal and Ontario Income Taxes (Figure 2)

Income taxes come into play at very low levels of earnings. Worse still, the income tax threshold is being steadily lowered each year as a result of Ottawa's decision in 1986 to partially index tax brackets and credits. For single persons in Ontario, federal and provincial income taxes begin at earnings of $7,000 and $9,000, respectively. These income tax thresholds are substantially below Statistics Canada's after-tax low-income cut-off of $12,867 for one person living in a metropolitan centre of 500,000 or more. Ontario's tax reduction raises its income tax thresh-

FIGURE 1
Marginal Tax Rate, Single Employable Person

Marginal tax rate (%)

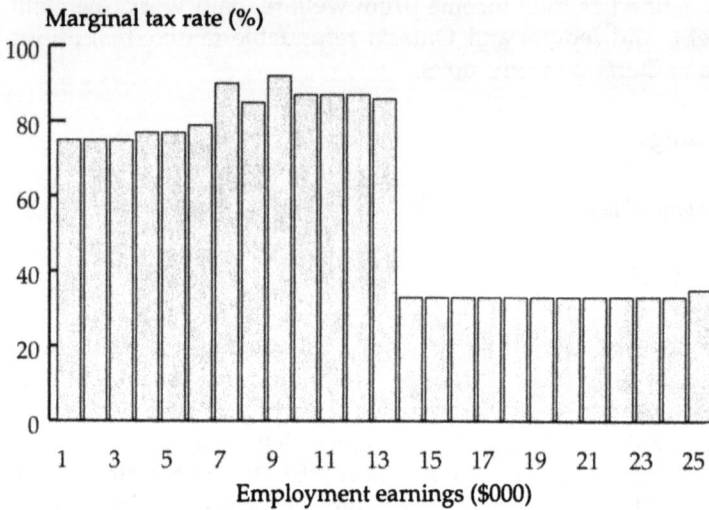

Employment earnings ($000)

Caledon Institute of Social Policy

FIGURE 2
Federal and Ontario Income Taxes, Single Employable Person

Income taxes

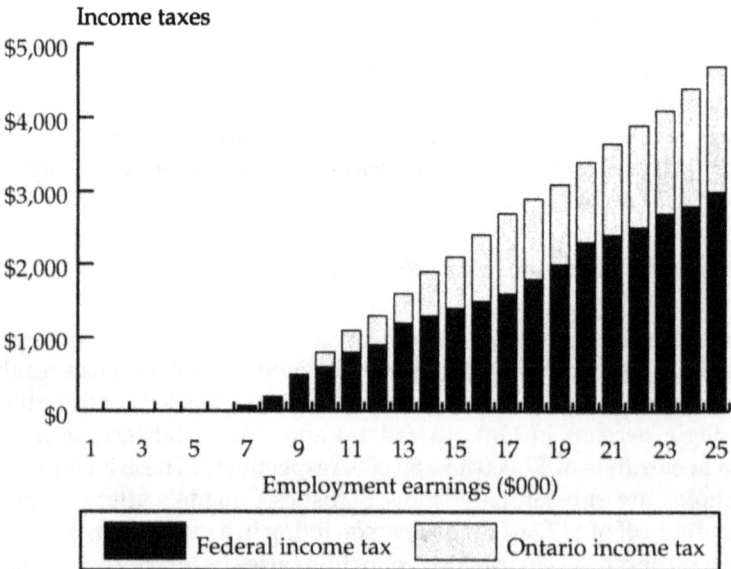

Employment earnings ($000)

Federal income tax   Ontario income tax

Caledon Institute of Social Policy

old somewhat relative to the federal income tax threshold; Ottawa got rid of its tax reduction in 1985.

The employment earnings level where federal income tax begins ($7,000) amounts to after-tax income of $10,944 for single employable persons on the STEP program or $1,923 below the $12,867 after-tax poverty line. Ontario income tax comes into play at $9,000 or after-tax income of $11,637 for single employable persons on STEP, which is still $1,230 below the poverty line.

Single employable welfare recipients with employment earnings of only $9,000 – where Ontario income tax begins – pay $423 in combined federal and Ontario income taxes. At $13,000 in earnings, when their after-tax income is $12,492 or almost exactly the after-tax low-income line of $12,867, they pay a hefty $1,579 in combined federal and Ontario income taxes, which amounts to an average tax rate of 11.2 per cent of their gross income.

Payroll Taxes (Figure 3)

Single employable welfare recipients begin to pay payroll taxes at just $4,000 in employment earnings. These taxes are small at first – only $19 in Canada Pension Plan (CPP) contributions at $4,000 – but rise suddenly and substantially to $403 in combined CPP contributions and unemployment insurance premiums at earnings of only $8,000. The jump is due to the introduction of unemployment insurance premiums between $7,000 and $8,000. Workers still eligible for some welfare benefits at earnings of $13,000 pay $703 in combined CPP contributions and UI premiums.

Welfare Benefits (Figure 4)

Figure 4 shows that welfare benefits are low and phase out rapidly as a result of the steep welfare taxback (since 75 per cent of earnings above a small flat-rate amount is effectively taxed through the reduction of welfare benefits). Single, employable persons with work earnings of $1,000 are eligible for a maximum of $7,797 in welfare benefits under General Welfare Assistance. At $13,000 in earnings, they may receive at most $508 in annual welfare payments; above that level, single workers are no longer eligible for social assistance. Workers earning $14,000 (and no longer eligible for a small amount of welfare under the STEP program) have an after-tax income of $12,720 – almost exactly the level of the after-tax low-income line of $12,867 for one person in

FIGURE 3
Payroll Taxes, Single Employable Person

CPP contributions and UI premiums

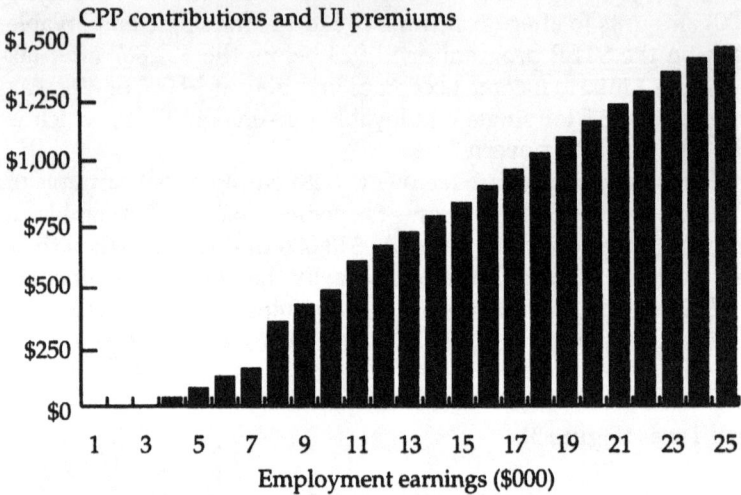

Employment earnings ($000)

Caledon Institute of Social Policy

FIGURE 4
Welfare Benefits, Single Employable Person

Welfare benefits

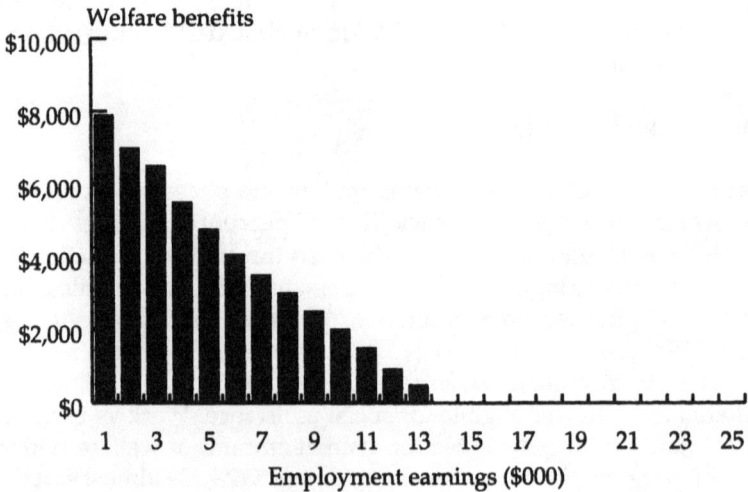

Employment earnings ($000)

Caledon Institute of Social Policy

a city of 500,000 or more. In other words, the welfare supplement for single employable workers ends at the poverty line.

Refundable Tax Credits (Figure 5)

The GST credit is worth a total of $246 at earnings of $1,000, composed of the maximum amount of the credit ($199 per adult) as well as $47 worth of the single person's supplement. The value of the supplement rises gradually with income until it peaks at $105. The GST credit reaches its maximum value of $304 ($199 basic and $105 supplement) at earnings of $10,000 and remains at that level until $25,000, above which it phases out and then disappears once earnings reach $30,000.

The Ontario property and sales tax credits, by contrast, decline steadily with income. Single employable persons receive $352 at $1,000 of earnings. Those still eligible for some welfare at earnings of $13,000 receive $258 in combined Ontario tax credits. The latter continue to decline until they are worth only $28 at $25,000 of earnings.

Disposable Income (Figure 6)

The graph on disposable income sums up the story clearly and simply. The disposable income of single employable recipients rises painfully slowly over the $1,000 to $13,000 earnings band. In fact, the "rise" is almost flat. It is only after workers move out of the welfare system (with employment earnings of about $14,000) that there is a noticeable and rapid improvement in disposable income.

Figure 6 shows visually the "weight" of the welfare system. Disposable income rises very slowly because most of the earnings from work are taxes – both directly through income and payroll taxes and indirectly through the welfare taxback and losses in the value of refundable tax credits. Again, the steep welfare taxback is the major brake on disposable income for the poorest workers. At earnings of $1,000, disposable income is $9,395; at $13,000, it comes to $11,789. *An extra $12,000 in work earnings (an increase of 1,200 per cent) yields only $2,394 more in disposable income (an increase of 25 per cent).*

Single-Parent Families, One Child Age 2

Marginal Tax Rate (Figure 7)

While the marginal tax rate for single-parent families follows a similar pattern to that of single employable persons, there are more ups and

FIGURE 5
Refundable Tax Credits, Single Employable Person

Refundable tax credits

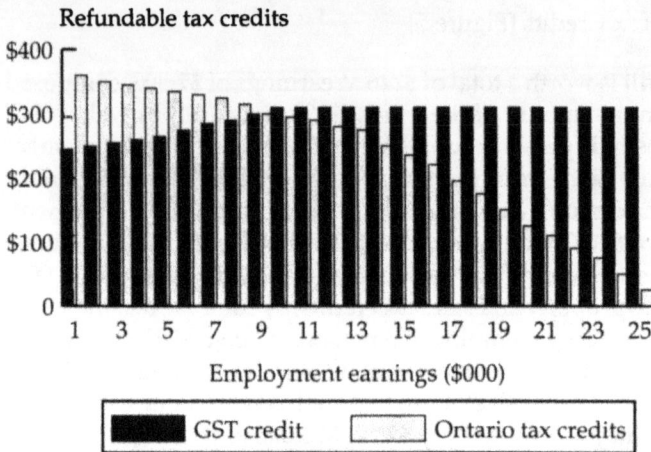

Caledon Institute of Social Policy

FIGURE 6
Disposable Income, Single Employable Person

Disposable income

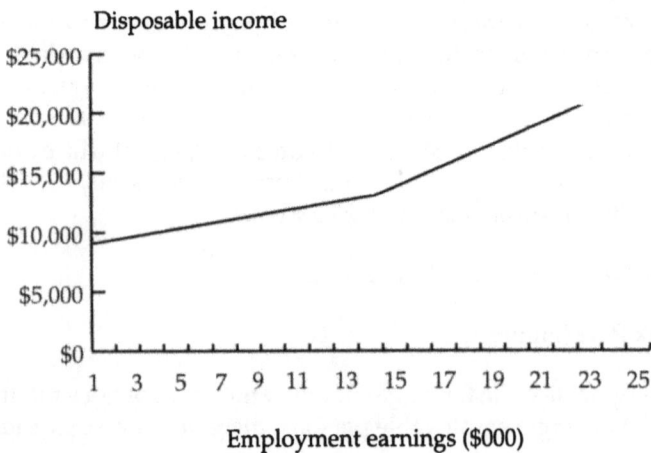

Caledon Institute of Social Policy

FIGURE 7
Marginal Tax Rate, Single Parent with One Child Age 2

Marginal tax rate (%)

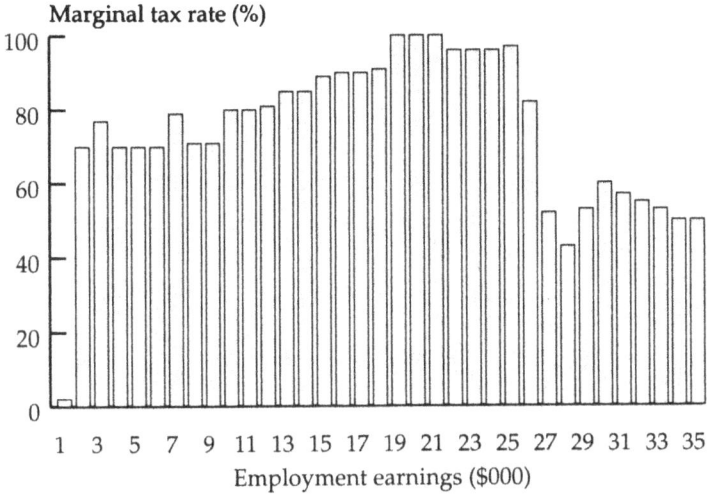

Employment earnings ($000)

Caledon Institute of Social Policy

FIGURE 8
Federal and Ontario Income Taxes, Single Parent with One Child Age 2

Income taxes

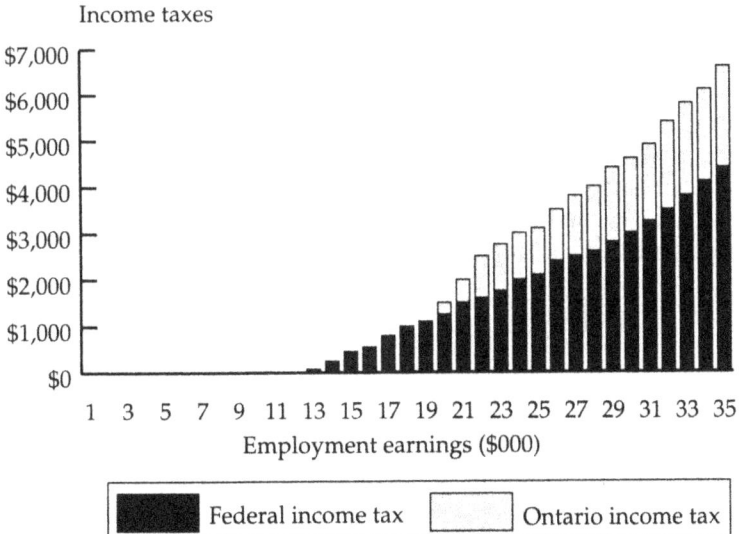

Employment earnings ($000)

| Federal income tax | Ontario income tax |

Caledon Institute of Social Policy

downs in figure 7. These wiggles are due to various benefits phasing in and out at different levels of earnings. Far more important, however, than the slightly erratic movement of the marginal tax rate is the fact that it is so very high – close to 100 per cent in some cases. This means that, *for every dollar of employment earnings, single parents on welfare lose almost a dollar through direct income and payroll taxes as well as indirect taxes in the form of the welfare taxback and loss of refundable credits.*

The marginal tax rate begins at just 2 per cent at $1,000 of employment earnings, rises to 68 per cent at earnings of $2,000 and 74 per cent at $3,000, and peaks at 95 per cent between earnings of $19,000 and $21,000. The marginal tax rate then eases to 89 per cent at earnings between $22,000 and $24,000. It drops sharply to 78 per cent at $26,000 and even farther to 46 per cent at earnings of $27,000 and 41 per cent at $28,000. The steep decline in the marginal tax rate is due to the fact that welfare phases out over a $3,000 earnings band between $24,000 and $27,000. The marginal tax rate rises to 47 per cent at $29,000 and 55 per cent at $30,000 as the GST credit and Ontario tax credits fall off rapidly.

Federal and Ontario Income Taxes (Figure 8)

Federal income tax starts at earnings of $13,000, which for this family corresponds to an after-tax income of $22,410 or $4,963 above the after-tax poverty line of $17,447 for two persons living in a metropolitan centre. The Ontario income tax threshold is $19,000 in earnings or $23,707 in after-tax income ($6,260 above the poverty line), which is far more generous than the federal threshold. The gap between the federal and Ontario tax thresholds is wider for families with children than for single people because the Ontario tax reduction provides a children's benefit, which is also significantly more generous than the adult benefit ($375 per child as opposed to $175 per adult). Figure 8 shows that income taxes rise steadily after the Ontario income tax system kicks in at earnings of $19,000.

Payroll Taxes (Figure 9)

Like single employable persons, single-parent welfare recipients begin to pay payroll taxes (CPP contributions) at $4,000 in employment earnings. Payroll taxes start at the same point for all households because these taxes are a function of employment earnings rather than family size. Again, payroll taxes are relatively small at first – only $19 at $4,000

FIGURE 9
Payroll Taxes, Single Parent with One Child Age 2

CPP contributions and UI premiums

Employment earnings ($000)

Caledon Institute of Social Policy

FIGURE 10
Welfare Benefits, Single Parent with One Child Age 2

Welfare benefits

Employment earnings ($000)

Caledon Institute of Social Policy

– but rise suddenly and substantially to reach $408 at $8,000 in earnings. The increase is due to the introduction of unemployment insurance premiums between $7,000 and $8,000. Single-parent families still theoretically eligible for some welfare benefits under STEP at earnings of $26,000 pay $1,506 in UI premiums and CPP contributions.

Welfare Benefits (Figure 10)

Single-parent families with one child age 2 and earning $1,000 are eligible for a maximum of $14,600 in welfare assistance from the Family Benefits program. At $26,000 in earnings, they get at most annual welfare benefits of only $371. At earnings of $27,000, they no longer are eligible for any welfare; this amounts to an after-tax income of $25,021, which is $7,574 above the after-tax low-income cut-off of $17,447.

Refundable Tax Credits (Figure 11)

The GST credit is worth a total of $503 at earnings of $1,000. This represents the maximum amount of the credit ($199 per adult and $199 for the first child in single-parent families) as well as the earned supplement of $105. Figure 11 shows that these families receive the maximum value of the GST credit up to earnings of $25,000 ($25,921 in net family income is the cut-off for the maximum benefit), after which the credit drops sharply.

The Ontario property and sales tax credits decline steadily across the earnings range shown in figure 11. Single-parent families receive $323 at $1,000 in employment earnings. Those still eligible for some social assistance at earnings of $26,000 get $107 in combined Ontario tax credits. These credits decline steadily until they are worth only $35 at $30,000 in earnings, above which they disappear.

Federal Child Tax Benefit (Figure 12)

Families earning between $1,000 and $3,000 receive the maximum basic child tax benefit for one child under age 7, which comes to $1,233 for the year (it is paid on a monthly basis). Families earning $4,000 get a bit more ($1,253) because the earned-income supplement for the working poor starts to phase in.

At $10,000, the combined benefit reaches its maximum $1,733 ($1,233 for the child tax credit and $500 for the earned-income supplement)

FIGURE 11
Refundable Tax Credits, Single Parent with One Child Age 2

Refundable tax credits

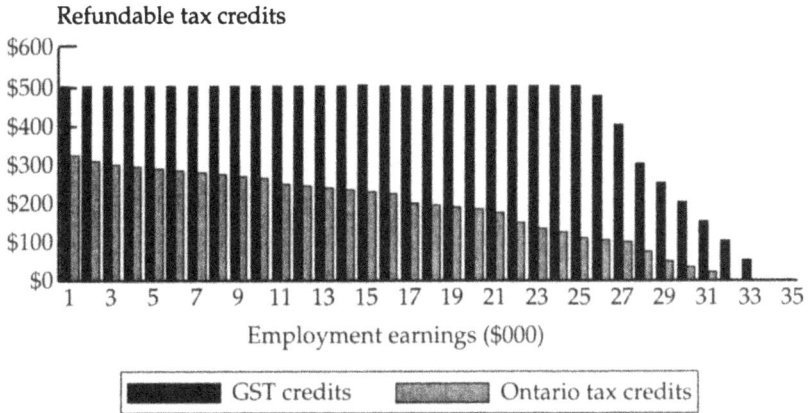

Employment earnings ($000)

GST credits   Ontario tax credits

Caledon Institute of Social Policy

FIGURE 12
Federal Child Tax Benefit, Single Parent with One Child Age 2

Child tax benefit

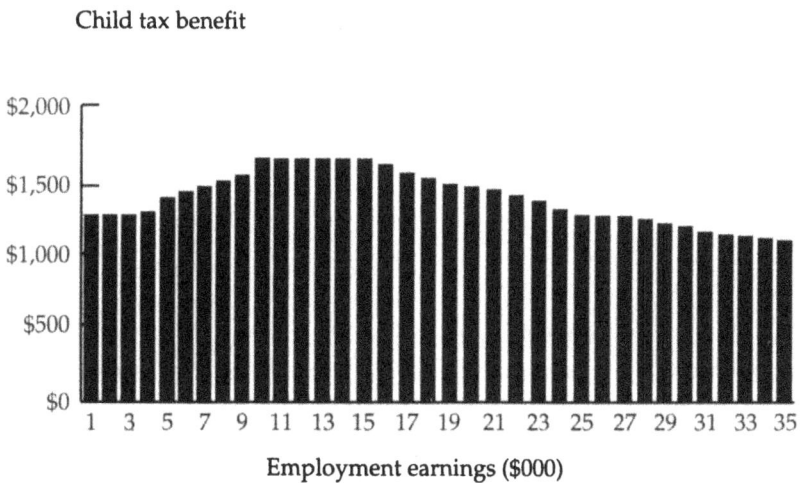

Employment earnings ($000)

Caledon Institute of Social Policy

and remains at this level until earnings of $15,000, above which first the earned-income supplement and later the basic credit decline steadily. At $30,000 in earnings, these families get $1,131 – only $102 less than families earning $3,000 or less.

Disposable Income (Figure 13)

The disposable income picture for single-parent families is much the same as for single employable persons. The point at which disposable income "takes off" is on the right-hand side of figure 13 for one-parent families, rather than mid-way as in figure 6 for single employable persons, only because the latter figure includes a wider range of earnings above the point where welfare disappears.) Figure 13 shows that the disposable income of single-parent welfare recipients rises consistently, but again very slowly, over the $1,000 to $26,000 earnings band. Once again, the "rise" is almost flat, indicating that the impact of work earnings upon total disposable income is marginal; most of the pay is lost to direct and indirect taxes, above all the welfare taxback.

At $1,000 in employment earnings, disposable income is $17,659. At $13,000 in earnings, disposable income is $21,697 – only $4,038 more in disposable income compared with the $12,000 increase in earnings. At $26,000 in earnings, disposable income is $23,230 – only $5,571 more than the $1,000 family despite a $25,000 increase in earnings. Between $13,000 and $26,000, doubling earnings nets a mere $1,533 improvement in take-home income. Overall, *a 2,500 per cent rise in earnings (i.e., from $1,000 to $26,000) results in a 32 per cent gain in disposable income.*

Moreover, the disposable income of single-parent families would be even lower if they had to pay for child care. As noted earlier, we assumed that these families would have access to fully subsidized child care because of their low levels of income.

Summary of Key Findings

Our analysis of nine other households found similar results. Welfare recipients pay very high marginal tax rates for low levels of earnings – typically in the 80 per cent to 95 per cent range. Recipients who supplement their benefits by working get to keep only a very small fraction of their earnings. Marginal tax rates drop sharply when households no longer are eligible for welfare assistance, indicating the substantial negative impact of the welfare taxback. The welfare taxback is

FIGURE 13
Disposable Income, Single Parent with One Child Age 2

Disposable income

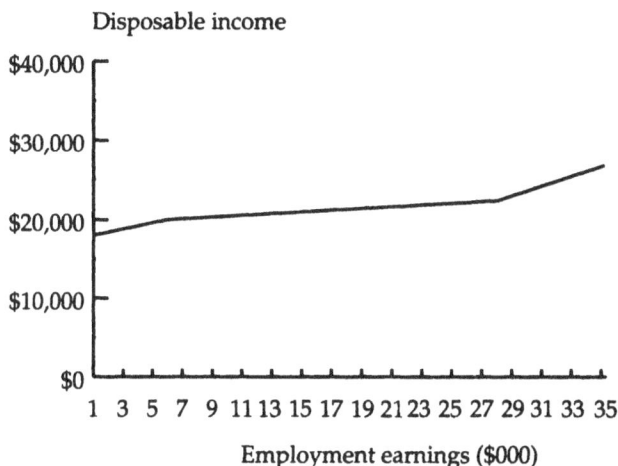

Employment earnings ($000)

Caledon Institute of Social Policy

the heaviest part of the tax burden imposed on welfare recipients who supplement their social assistance by working in the labour force.

Federal and provincial income taxes start at very low levels of earnings, which is a significant burden for the working poor. The Ontario tax reduction eases the tax burden on the poor to some extent by raising the taxpaying threshold for provincial income tax, especially for families with children.

Once we factor in welfare benefits (which are not subject to income tax) paid to households in the STEP program, the picture looks quite different. Both federal and Ontario income taxes begin substantially *below* the poverty line for single employable persons on welfare; the federal income tax threshold begins at after-tax income of $10,944, or $1,923 below the poverty line, and the Ontario tax threshold is set at after-tax income of $11,637, or $1,230 under the poverty line. However, federal and Ontario income taxes come into effect at after-tax incomes that are *above* the poverty line for one-parent families and two-earner couples with children who supplement their welfare benefits by working for pay.

Payroll taxes in the form of Canada Pension Plan contributions and unemployment insurance premiums start at very low levels of earnings. The fact that they flatten out after earnings of $33,000 and higher for each paid worker makes these payroll taxes regressive in their impact overall.

While disposable income rises steadily with increased earnings for all households, the actual gain is marginal. Welfare recipients pay back to government most of their employment earnings – mainly in the form of the welfare taxback, but also in income and payroll taxes and lost refundable credits. For welfare recipients entering or re-entering the labour market, the cost of working is very high.

Exploration of Options

The Welfare System

The analysis of the interaction of the welfare and tax/transfer systems found that most of the total tax burden is represented by the welfare taxback. Accordingly, we tested several options that attempt to reduce the burden of this taxback. The options involve changing the value of the flat-rate and variable components of the earnings exemption currently in place under STEP.

While the study conducted for the Ontario Fair Tax Commission explored six options for reducing the tax burden in the welfare category alone, only two possible options are presented here for illustrative purposes.

Option 1: Double Flat-Rate Exemption (Figures 14–15)

Under the first option, the flat-rate component of the earnings exemption permitted under STEP was doubled from $75 to $150 per person. Figure 14 shows that this increase slightly improves disposable income for single employable welfare recipients earning between $1,000 and $15,000. (Disposable income refers to total income from welfare, work, child benefits, and federal and provincial refundable tax credits, minus payroll taxes and federal and provincial income taxes.)

Because a flat-rate exemption affects all recipients equally, the increase to this component of the exemption provides a small benefit to them all. However, the percentage increase is larger at the bottom end of the earnings scale because these people lose fewer welfare benefits to the variable exemption on earnings. In addition to increasing disposable income, the rise in the flat-rate exemption has the effect of pushing out the earnings threshold within which recipients still are eligible for some social assistance from $13,000 to $15,000.

FIGURE 14
Disposable Income, Single Employable Person,
Option 1 – Double Flat-Rate Exemption

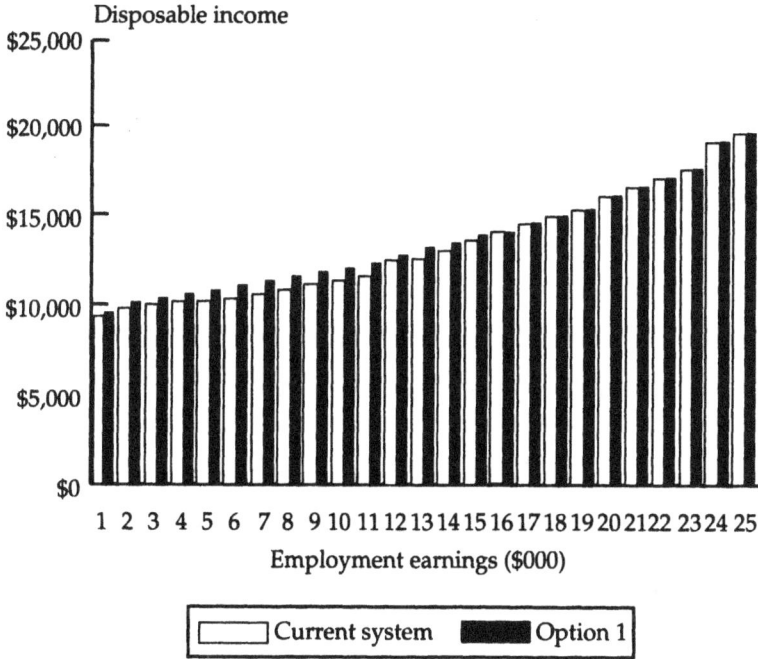

Disposable income

Employment earnings ($000)

Current system   Option 1

Caledon Institute of Social Policy

FIGURE 15
Marginal Tax Rate, Single Employable Person,
Option 1 – Double Flat-Rate Exemption

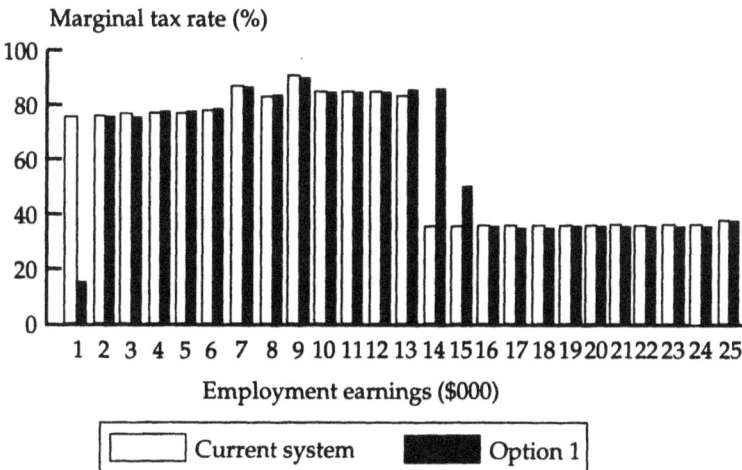

Marginal tax rate (%)

Employment earnings ($000)

Current system   Option 1

Caledon Institute of Social Policy

Figure 15 shows the impact of this option on marginal tax rates, defined as one minus the increase in disposable income between two earnings levels divided by the increase in earnings. Despite the rise in disposable income, the change in marginal tax rates in the earnings range within which single employable recipients still qualify for welfare (between earnings of $1,000 and $15,000) is almost imperceptible – except at the $1,000 earnings level where the larger flat-rate exemption cancels out the welfare taxback entirely, producing a marginal tax rate of only 15 per cent. Even though disposable income may be higher, the percentage increase in disposable income between earnings levels in most instances is equivalent to the current system – resulting in the same marginal tax rate. Beyond $15,000, the marginal tax rate drops significantly anyway because eligibility for welfare ends.

Raising the flat-rate component of the exemption represents one method of increasing disposable income at the very low end of the earnings scale. In order to reduce work disincentives for welfare recipients with higher earnings, options that target the variable component of the exemption would be more appropriate.

Option 2: Lower Variable Exemption (Figures 16–17)

While the study conducted for the Ontario Fair Tax Commission tested five options for lowering the variable component of the earnings exemption, only one example is presented here. In Option 2, the variable component of the earnings exemption was lowered from its existing 75 per cent to 67 per cent. Reducing the variable exemption from 75 per cent to 67 per cent increases disposable income by several hundred dollars, as illustrated in figure 16, which compares Option 2 and the current system.

The pattern is similar in magnitude to the first option, except that Option 2 is relatively more generous for recipients with higher earnings; the largest percentage increase in disposable income is seven per cent for recipients earning $14,000. Because variable exemptions are set as a percentage of earnings, they are worth more to recipients with higher earnings.

As in doubling the flat-rate exemption, lowering the variable exemption from 75 to 67 per cent has the effect of pushing out the threshold within which single employable persons still may qualify for welfare from earnings of $13,000 under the current system to $16,000 under Option 2.

Figure 17 shows that the marginal tax rate, for the most part, is lower

FIGURE 16
Disposable Income, Single Employable Person,
Option 2 – Lower Variable Exemption from 75% to 67%

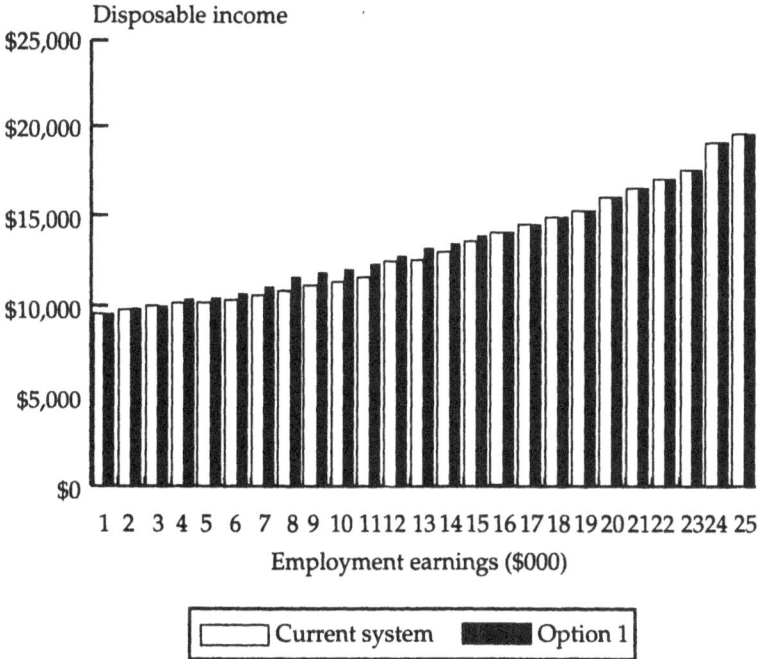

Caledon Institute of Social Policy

FIGURE 17
Marginal Tax Rate, Single Employable Person,
Option 2 – Lower Variable Exemption from 75% to 67%

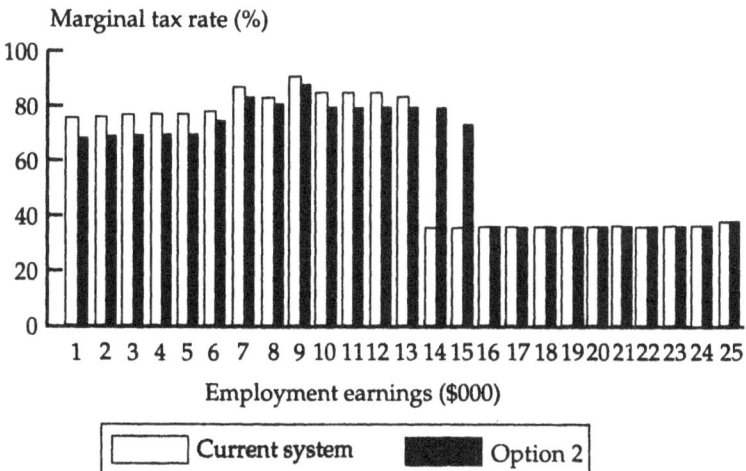

Caledon Institute of Social Policy

under Option 2 than under the current system because of the lower welfare taxback. However, it increases significantly at the $14,000 and $15,000 earnings band, reflecting the fact that the greatest proportion of the tax burden – the welfare taxback – now applies to those bands.

Option 2 is more targeted than Option 1 because the former results in a smaller increase in disposable income and also concentrates its largest benefits on a more narrow earnings range. Lowering the variable exemption is a more appropriate option for removing some of the disincentive to work.

The results point to the problems associated with devising options for reform that are framed solely upon an assessment of marginal tax rates, the classic measure of the tax burden. While the marginal tax rates of persons in the lower earnings bands increase, their disposable income increases as well. The analysis makes clear the importance of looking at several measures, especially disposable income, in assessing possible options for reform.

Federal Tax/Transfers

Because all provincial income taxes, except those in Quebec, are calculated as a percentage of federal income tax, the study explored possible changes to the federal tax/transfer system (i.e., the base for the Ontario income tax system).

Option 3: Progressive Income Tax Schedule (Figures 18–19)

In Option 3, federal income tax rates were changed to correspond to those in place prior to the 1988 federal tax reform; the latter reduced the number of tax brackets from ten to three and lowered the top marginal tax rate. We updated to 1992 dollars the tax brackets to which these rates applied. The following tax rates and corresponding brackets were incorporated in the Caledon Tax/Transfer Model: 6 per cent on taxable income under $1,632; 16 per cent on taxable income between $1,633 and $3,262; 17 per cent on $3,263–$6,252; 18 per cent on $6,253–$9,787; 19 per cent on $9,788–$16,311; 20 per cent on $16,312–$22,836; 23 per cent on $22,837–$29,361; 25 per cent on $29,362–$45,673; 30 per cent on $45,674–$78,297; and 34 per cent on taxable income of $78,298 or more.

The results in figures 18 and 19 show that the effect of this change at the lower end of the earnings scale is negligible because the lower tax rates are applied to very low levels of earnings. Most of the burden

FIGURE 18
Disposable Income, Single Employable Person,
Option 3 – Progressive Income Tax Schedule

Disposable income

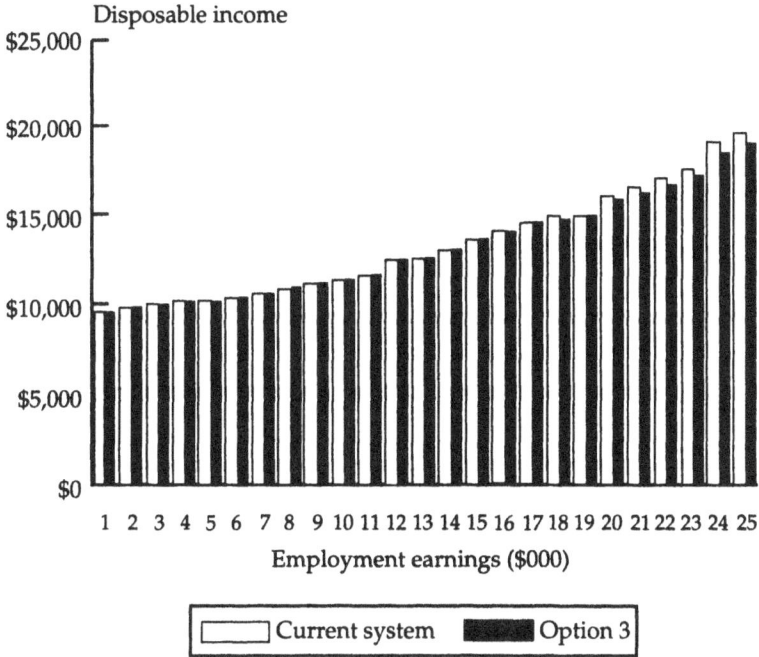

Caledon Institute of Social Policy

FIGURE 19
Marginal Tax Rate, Single Employable Person,
Option 3 – Progressive Income Tax Schedule

Marginal tax rate (%)

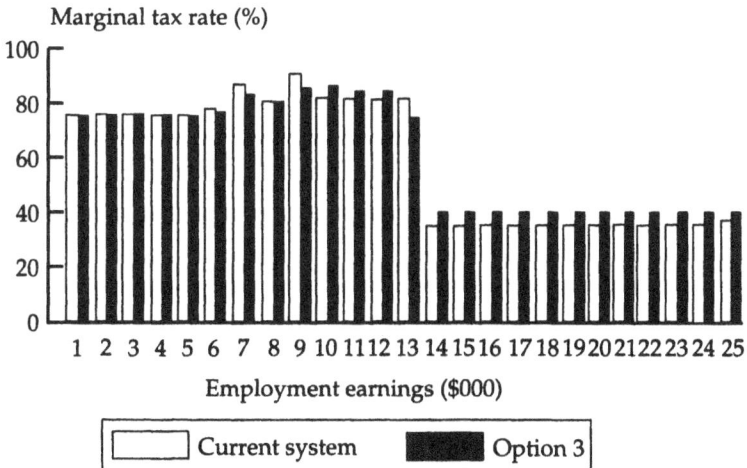

Caledon Institute of Social Policy

of total taxes on welfare recipients who supplement their benefits by working for wages derives from the welfare taxback, not federal and provincial income taxes.

Option 4: Federal Low-Income Tax Credit (Figures 20–1)

The second option in this category involves the removal of federal income tax from single employable persons on STEP under the relevant after-tax poverty line ($12,867) – in this case, up to and including after-tax income of $13,000, or $11,000 in employment earnings.

Federal income tax was removed by introducing a non-refundable tax credit equal to the amount of federal income tax up to a maximum value of $700, which is equivalent to federal income tax at earnings of $11,000. The threshold for the maximum credit is $13,000 in after-tax family income. The credit declines at a rate of 10 per cent above the threshold, disappearing at earnings of $20,000. For example, workers earning $9,000 owe $370 in federal income tax and so would get a credit of $370, removing the federal income tax burden. Those earning $11,000 have federal income tax of $704 and would qualify for the maximum credit of $700, leaving $4 owing. Workers earnings $15,000 pay federal income tax of $1,372 and would qualify for a credit of $500, leaving federal income tax payable of $872.

We propose a family rather than an individual definition of income for purposes of the low-income tax credits proposed in our study, for both cost and equity reasons. Using an individual definition of income would result in low-wage individuals in non-poor families receiving the low-income tax credit, whereas higher-wage workers in non-poor families with the same total income would not be eligible for the low-income tax credit. Obviously costs would rise as well if the low-income tax credit were based on individual as opposed to family income. Statistics Canada's low-income cut-offs, which we used to establish the thresholds for our low-income tax credit, are based on family – not individual – income.

Figures 20 and 21 show that this option provides modest assistance to households in the $7,000 to $19,000 earnings band, with maximum help being directed to those earning between $14,000 and $16,000. This represents a targeted option in that it directs assistance primarily toward recipients on the margins of the welfare system.

FIGURE 20
Disposable Income, Single Employable Person,
Option 4 – Federal Low-Income Tax Credit

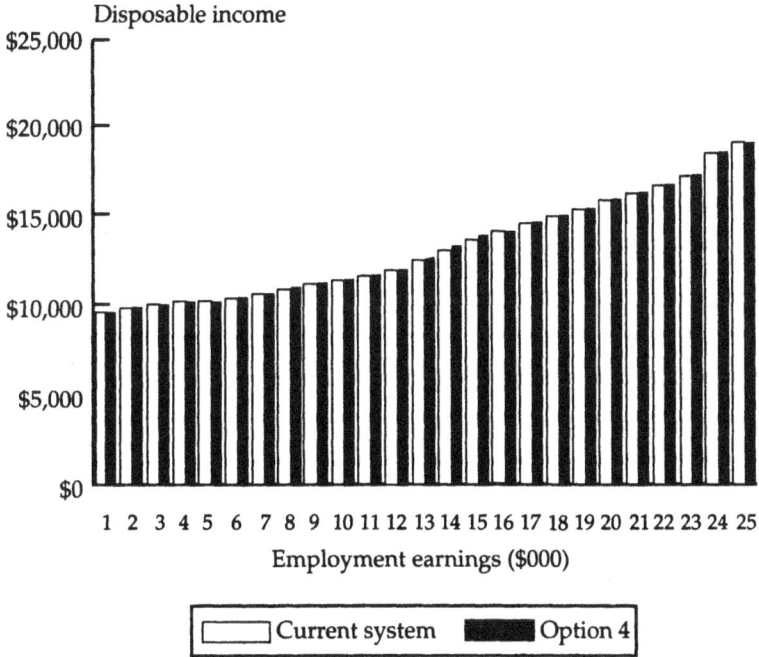

Caledon Institute of Social Policy

FIGURE 21
Marginal Tax Rate, Single Employable Person,
Option 4 – Federal Low-Income Tax Credit

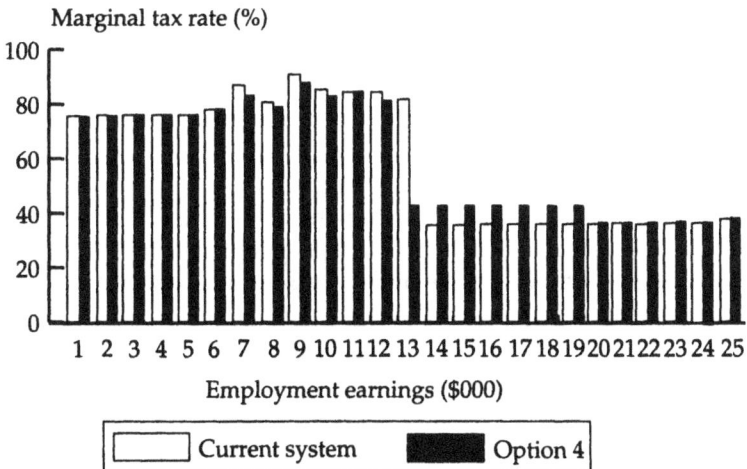

Caledon Institute of Social Policy

Option 5: Tax Welfare (Figures 22–3)

The third option in this category is almost the opposite of the second. Rather than eliminating income tax for low-income persons, welfare was counted as taxable income. The deduction of federal and provincial income taxes currently permitted under STEP was not allowed and both welfare and employment earnings were considered to be taxable income.

The purpose of testing this option was to determine what would happen if all sources of income were treated equally – i.e., "a buck is a buck is a buck," welfare included. This would remove the current disparity between the tax treatment of the welfare poor and the working poor.

The results show that, of all the options considered here, only this one has a serious negative impact upon disposable income. Figure 22 shows that disposable incomes for single employable recipients under Option 5 are lower than under the current system – a not insignificant loss of between seven and nine per cent of disposable income for certain households.

The marginal tax rate for the $1,000 to $7,000 earnings band is higher than under the current system because recipients in this band formerly were exempt from taxation. Above these earnings, the marginal tax rate is almost identical because earnings at higher levels already are subject to income tax.

This option could not be implemented on its own. It would have to be combined with some other measure – either a reduced welfare taxback and/or a low-income tax credit in order to offset the tax burden that would be created by this move toward equity between working poor Ontarians with and without a welfare supplement from STEP. An example of an approach that combines taxation of welfare with a lower welfare taxback and a low-income tax credit is considered in Option 11.

Option 6: Double Basic GST Credit (Figures 24–5)

The last option in the federal tax/transfer system was to boost the refundable GST credit. In this case, the value of the basic component of the GST credit was doubled from $199 per person to $400 per person. The design of the current credit (i.e., its thresholds and reduction rates) was retained.

The impact of this impact upon marginal tax rates and disposable

FIGURE 22
Disposable Income, Single Employable Person,
Option 5 – Tax Welfare

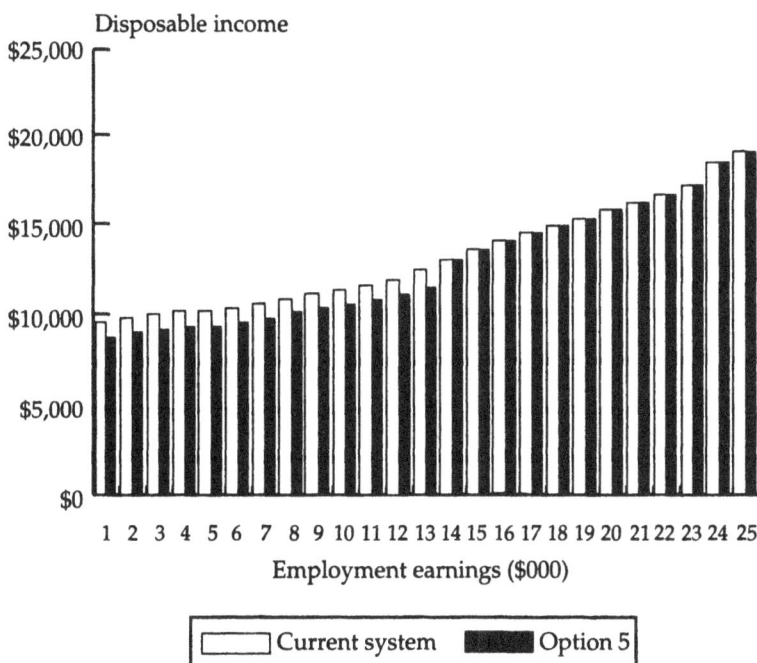

Caledon Institute of Social Policy

FIGURE 23
Marginal Tax Rate, Single Employable Person,
Option 5 – Tax Welfare

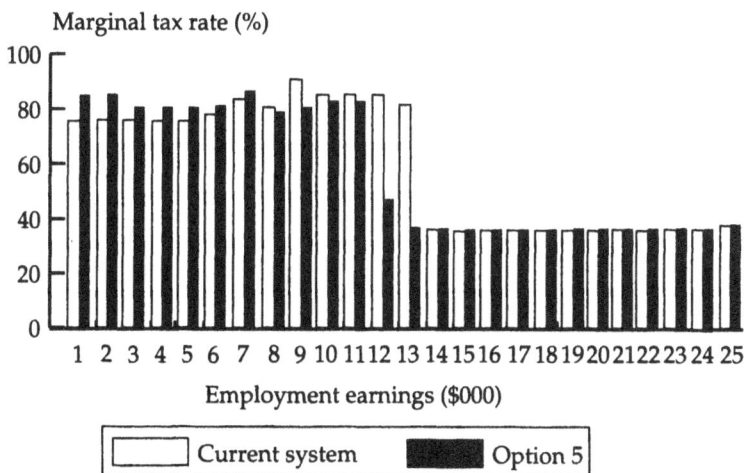

Caledon Institute of Social Policy

FIGURE 24
Disposable Income, Single Employable Person,
Option 6 – Double Basic GST Credit

Disposable income

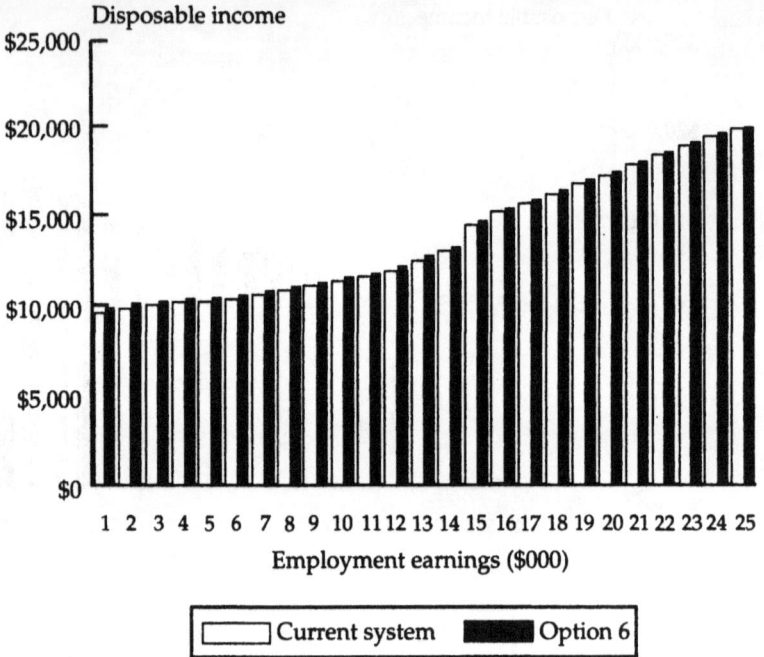

Employment earnings ($000)

Current system   Option 6

Caledon Institute of Social Policy

FIGURE 25
Marginal Tax Rate, Single Employable Person,
Option 6 –Double Basic GST Credit

Marginal tax rate (%)

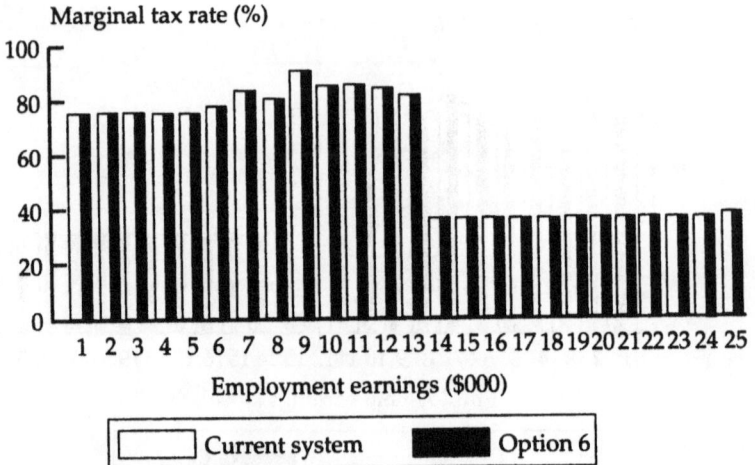

Employment earnings ($000)

Current system   Option 6

Caledon Institute of Social Policy

income is negligible. The increase ranges from just two per cent at the bottom end of the earnings scale to one per cent at $25,000. While the impact of this option is relatively small, it affects households over a wide range of earnings because of the low (five per cent) reduction rate built into the credit. In order to have a real effect on disposable income, the value of the GST credit would have to increase much more.

This option would have high cost implications because it would apply to all lower-income and many modest-income Canadians and not simply to recipients of welfare. Moreover, it might be seen by some as an inappropriate means of combating poverty because the GST credit is not intended to act more generally as an income supplement, but rather only to partially offset the amount of GST that lower-income households must pay.

Ontario Tax/Transfers

Four options with respect to Ontario income taxes and transfers were modelled; the results of three of these options are presented here.

Option 7: Double Ontario Tax Reduction (Figures 26–7)

In Option 7, we raised the Ontario income tax threshold by doubling the Ontario tax reduction from $175 to $350. The improvements were almost imperceptible and provided only a sliver of assistance to single employable welfare recipients in a very narrow earnings band (between $9,000 and $12,000). The major effect of doubling the Ontario tax reduction is to push up the starting point for Ontario taxes from $9,000 to $11,000. The impact of this option, however, is much more significant for families with children (discussed later).

Option 8: Ontario Low-Income Tax Credit (Figures 28–9)

In Option 8, we removed Ontario income tax entirely from persons in the welfare band ($1,000 to $13,000). The tax was removed by introducing a credit worth a maximum $400 – just over the $367 in Ontario income tax that single employable persons pay at $11,000 in employment earnings or $13,000 in after-tax family income, which is roughly equivalent to the poverty line. (We also modelled an enriched low-income tax credit.) The Ontario low-income tax credit is reduced at a rate of 10 per cent above the threshold of $13,000 in after-tax family

FIGURE 26
Disposable Income, Single Employable Person,
Option 7 – Double Ontario Tax Reduction

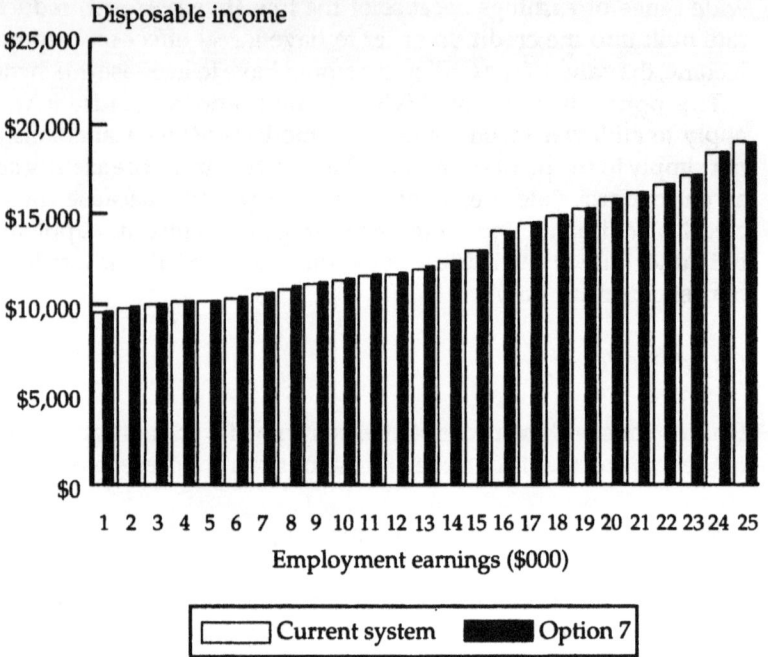

Disposable income

[Bar chart. Y-axis: $0 to $25,000 in $5,000 increments. X-axis: Employment earnings ($000) from 1 to 25. Two series: Current system and Option 7.]

Employment earnings ($000)

| Current system | Option 7 |

Caledon Institute of Social Policy

FIGURE 27
Marginal Tax Rate, Single Employable Person,
Option 7 –Double Ontario Tax Reduction

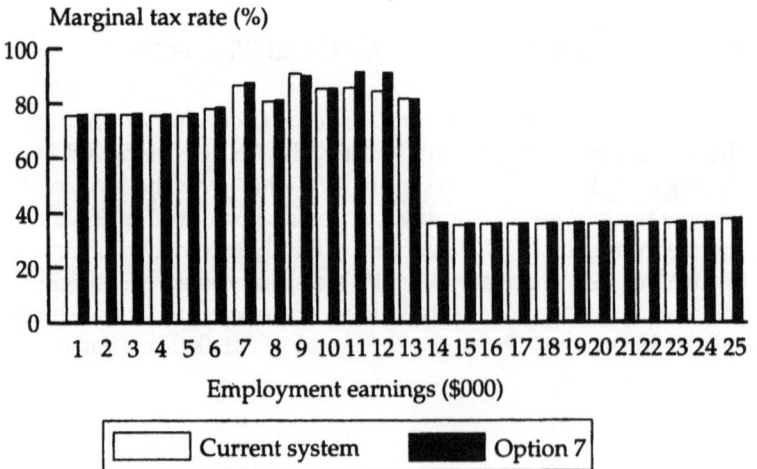

Marginal tax rate (%)

[Bar chart. Y-axis: 0 to 100 in increments of 20. X-axis: Employment earnings ($000) from 1 to 25. Two series: Current system and Option 7.]

Employment earnings ($000)

| Current system | Option 7 |

Caledon Institute of Social Policy

FIGURE 28
Disposable Income, Single Employable Person,
Option 8 – Ontario Low-Income Tax Credit

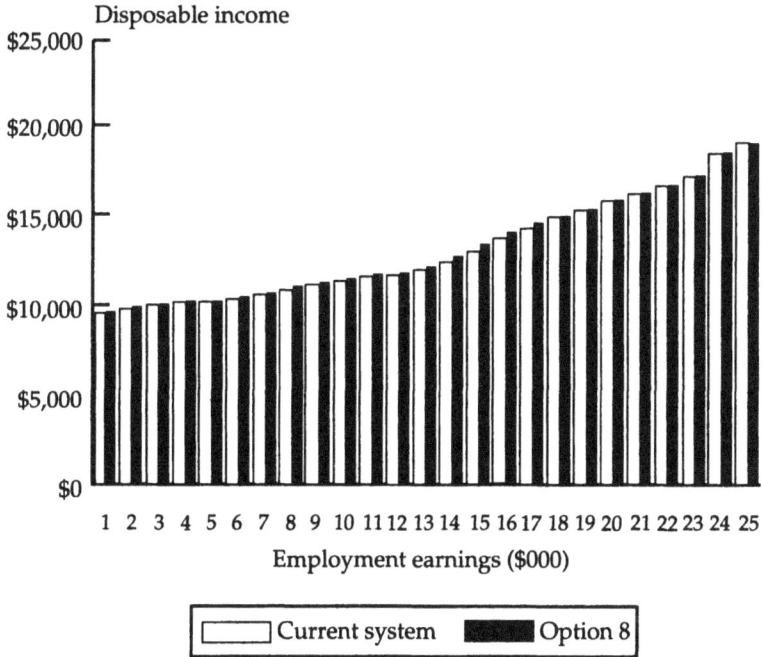

Caledon Institute of Social Policy

FIGURE 29
Marginal Tax Rate, Single Employable Person,
Option 8 – Ontario Low-Income Tax Credit

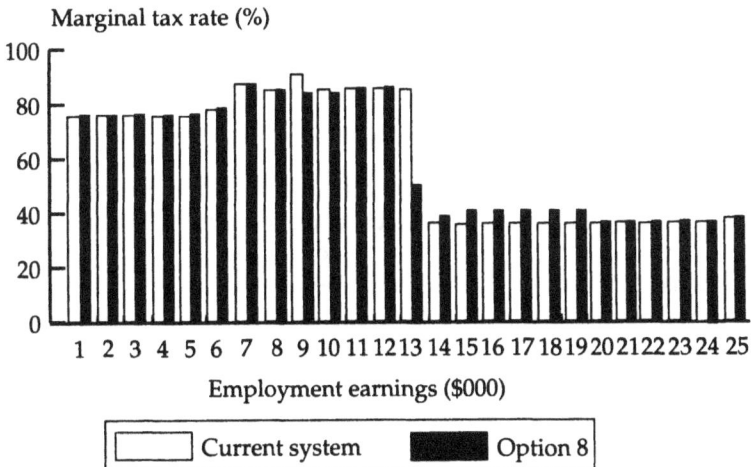

Caledon Institute of Social Policy

income and phases out at after-tax income of $17,000, which amounts in the case of single employable persons on STEP to earnings of $20,000.

Again, this option generated slight improvements in disposable income. There is only a small percentage increase in disposable income, with those in the $14,000 to $16,000 earnings band benefitting most. The credit does not help recipients below $9,000 in earnings because they do not pay any Ontario income tax.

Option 9: Double Ontario Sales Tax Credit (Figures 30–1)

As with the federal-only examples, we tested an option that focuses on the transfer rather than the tax side of the tax/transfer system. We doubled the value of the Ontario refundable sales tax credit from $100 per adult to $200 per adult. Current thresholds and reduction rates were retained.

Figure 30 makes clear that this option only slightly improves disposable income, the increases ranging from one per cent at $1,000 in earnings to a mere one-half of one per cent at $25,000. A much more generous credit would be required to have a discernible effect on disposable income and corresponding marginal tax rates. In general, improvements to existing Ontario refundable credits would have only a slight impact because the credits extend relatively far up the earnings scale and do not target their assistance toward households with very low earnings.

There are significant cost implications associated with this option and, more generally, with any form of low-income tax credit. The higher costs would arise not only from raising the value of the credit but also from the fact that all low-income Ontarians (and not simply welfare recipients) would benefit from this form of assistance. These costs could be offset through other changes to the income tax system, such as raising the top marginal tax rate and converting RRSP and RPP deductions to credits.

Combined Options

Each of the options in the above categories tested only a single variable in order to determine the impact represented by that one change. In seeking ways to reduce the tax burden on low-income households, it may be more appropriate to combine selected single options. In this way, moderate changes can be made to several of the components that comprise the tax burden. The desired results may be effected through

FIGURE 30
Disposable Income, Single Employable Person,
Option 9 – Double Ontario Sales Tax Credit

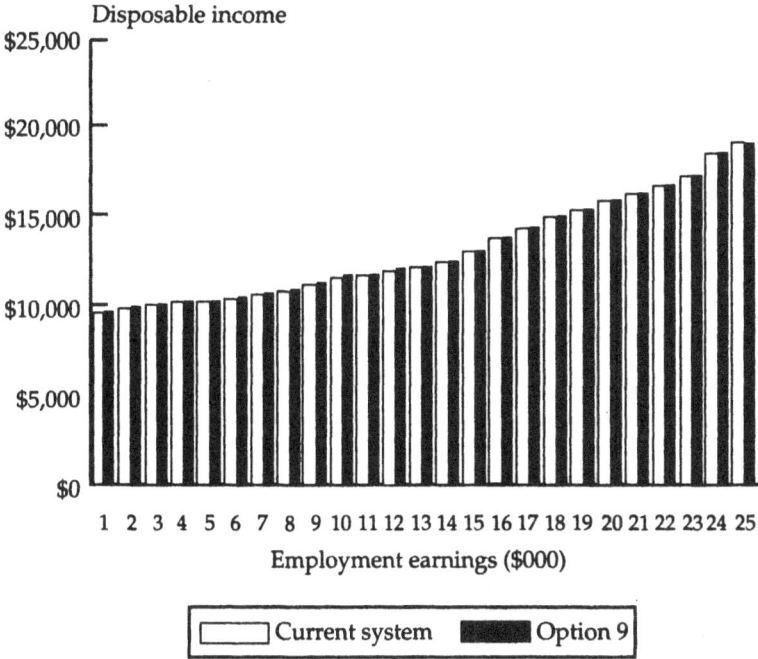

Caledon Institute of Social Policy

FIGURE 31
Marginal Tax Rate, Single Employable Person,
Option 9 – Double Ontario Sales Tax Credit

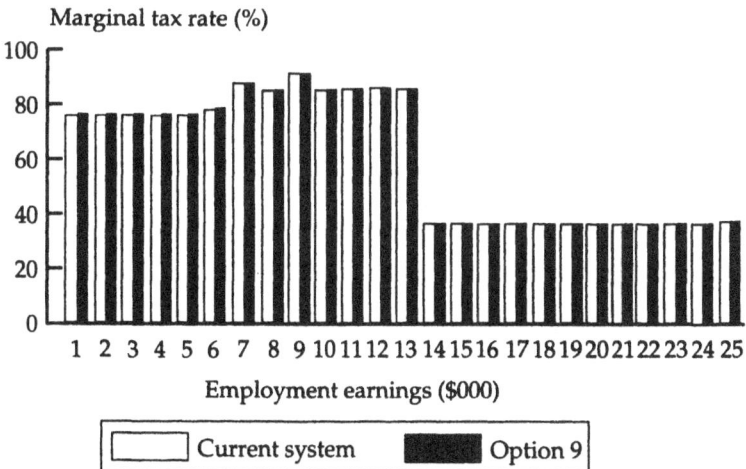

Caledon Institute of Social Policy

a combination of measures rather than through a substantial change to one element only that would have significant implications for cost or other factors, such as equity or eligibility for welfare.

For example, a modestly increased provincial sales tax credit combined with a slightly lower variable exemption on welfare could have the same effect as a very high boost in the sales tax credit. The former option would be less costly because only part would apply to all lower-income households. At the same time, it would open up the welfare system in that it would extend the band of earnings within which individuals still were eligible for welfare assistance, which would add to its cost.

While there are many possibilities, the results of only three combined options are presented here.

Option 10: Tax Welfare; Lower Variable Exemption (Figures 32–3)

Option 10 combines the taxation of welfare with a lower variable earnings exemption of 50 per cent (the existing rate is 75 per cent). The results show that the lower variable exemption on welfare does not compensate for the impact of income taxes at the low end of the earnings scale. Recipients earning between $1,000 and $8,000 would lose disposable income because they now would pay tax on income that formerly was exempt from taxation.

The combined effect of taxing welfare and a 50 per cent variable exemption on welfare pushes out the welfare threshold to $17,000 from its current cut-off of $13,000 in earnings. This is not as high, however, as the $22,000 earnings level that still qualifies for welfare under the single 50 per cent variable exemption, the results of which are presented in the full study submitted to the Ontario Fair Tax Commission.

The lower welfare threshold results from the taxation of welfare by changing the STEP formula, which calculates welfare on net earnings. The taxation of welfare tested in this option means that welfare is calculated on gross earnings. Even though the variable exemption is lower than under the current system, the taxback is high because the 50 per cent is based on gross earnings. The high taxback reduces welfare eligibility more quickly (i.e., at $17,000) than when the 50 per cent variable exemption is applied on its own.

FIGURE 32
Disposable Income, Single Employable Person,
Option 10 – Double Ontario Sales Tax Credit

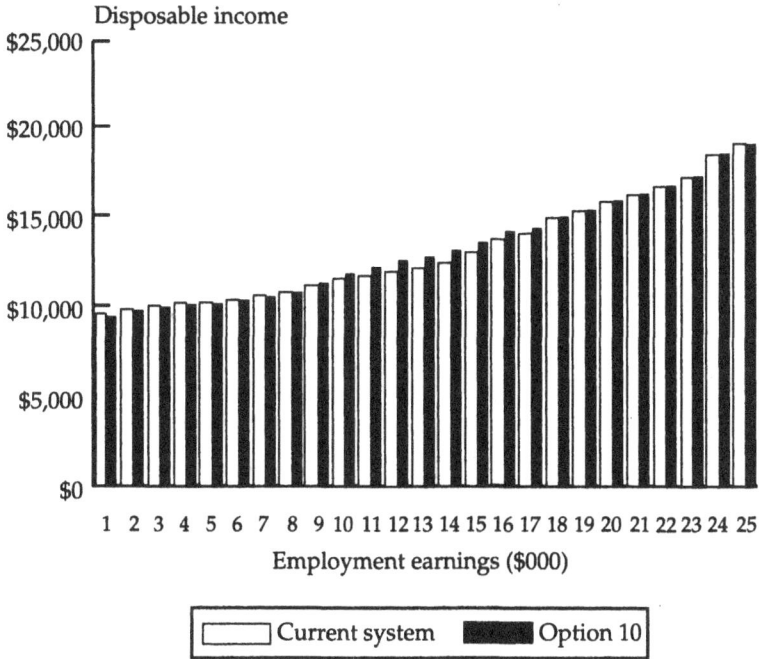

Caledon Institute of Social Policy

FIGURE 33
Marginal Tax Rate, Single Employable Person,
Option 10 – Tax Welfare/Lower Variable Exemption to 50%

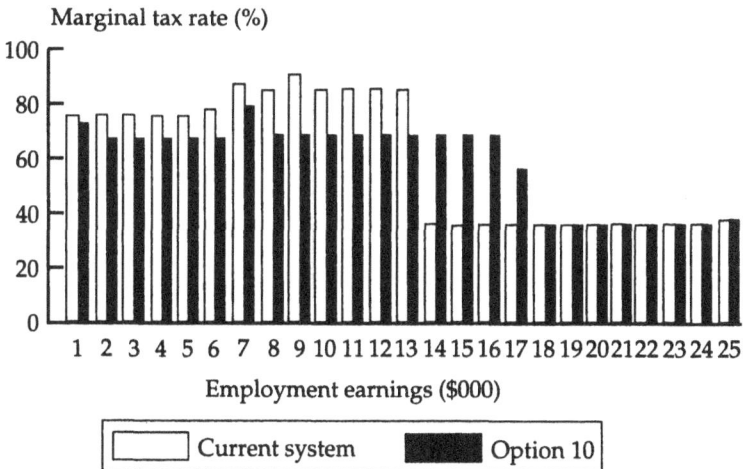

Caledon Institute of Social Policy

Option 11: Tax Welfare; Federal/Ontario Low-Income Tax Credit;
Lower Variable Exemption (Figures 34–5)

Option 11 combines a federal/Ontario low-income tax credit with a
lower variable earnings exemption of 67 per cent (from the existing 75
per cent) and taxation of welfare. The tax credit developed for this
option is a variant of the federal low-income credit devised in Option
4 and the Ontario low-income tax credit devised for Option 8. The
maximum credit was set at $1,100, payable at the threshold of $13,000
in after-tax family income (roughly the $12,867 after-tax poverty line
for one person in a city of 500,000 or more) where current income taxes
total $1,071. We used a reduction rate of 20 per cent so that the credit
is reasonably well targeted; it disappears at after-tax income of $18,500
or 44 per cent above the poverty line.

The results in Figures 34 show a significant though not large increase
in disposable income, especially for recipients earning between $9,000
and $16,000. The disposable income for these households increases by
between five and nine per cent.

The marginal tax rate for the earnings included in most of the "welfare band" drops somewhat with this option (figure 35). The variable
exemption is largely responsible for the improvement in that the federal and provincial income taxes within this income band comprise a
relatively small component of the tax burden compared with the welfare taxback. The marginal tax rate is higher for households with earnings between $11,000 and $21,000 because of the fairly steep (20 per
cent) reduction rate of the federal/Ontario low-income tax credit cou-
pled with the fact that the welfare taxback does not apply above earnings of $13,000.

Again, these results are instructive. Policy options framed solely on
the basis of marginal tax rates might reject this option because marginal
tax rates increase between earnings of $11,000 and $21,000. It is essen-
tial to balance this conventional criterion with a consideration of
percentage change in disposable income that shows important improvements for households over a wide range of earnings.

Option 12: Ontario Low-Income Tax Credit; Lower Variable
Exemption (Figures 36–7)

The third combined option consists of two Ontario actions – the
Ontario low-income tax credit tested in Option 8 (which removes
Ontario income tax from poor households) and the lower variable

FIGURE 34
Disposable Income, Single Employable Person,
Option 11 – Tax Welfare/Low-Income Tax Credit/Lower
Variable Exemption to 67%

Disposable income

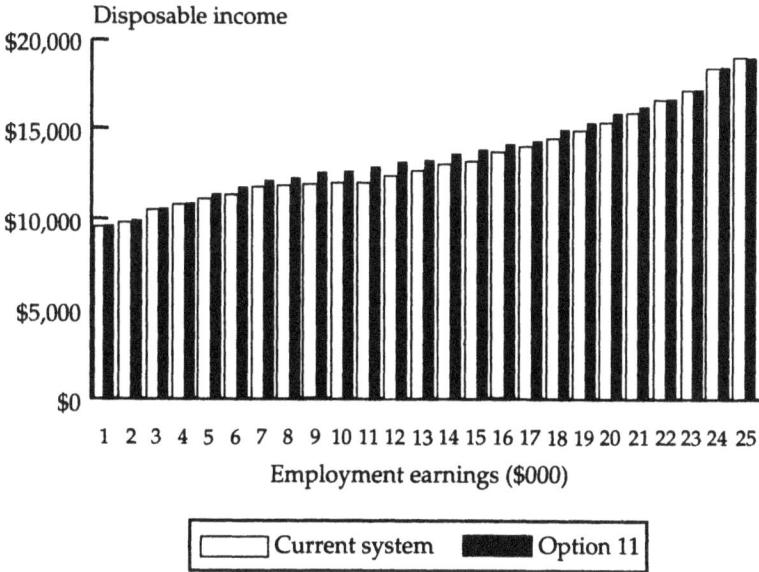

Employment earnings ($000)

Current system   Option 11

Caledon Institute of Social Policy

FIGURE 35
Marginal Tax Rate, Single Employable Person,
Option 11 – Tax Welfare/Low-Income Tax Credit/Lower
Variable Exemption to 67%

Marginal tax rate (%)

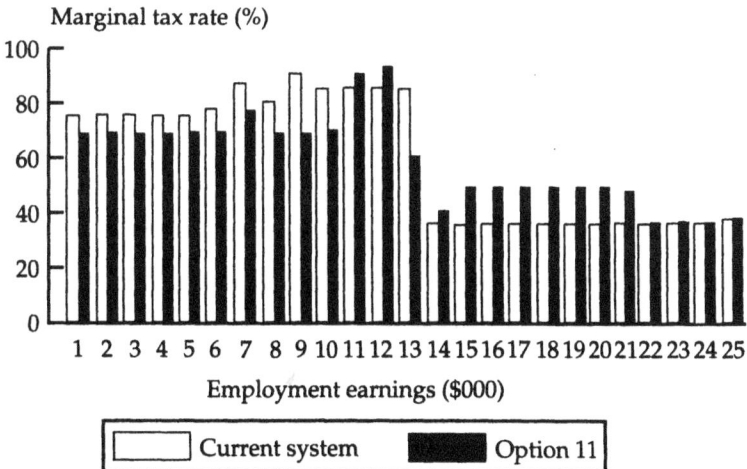

Employment earnings ($000)

Current system   Option 11

Caledon Institute of Social Policy

FIGURE 36
Disposable Income, Single Employable Person,
Option 12 – Ontario Low-Income Tax Credit/Lower Variable
Exemption to 67%

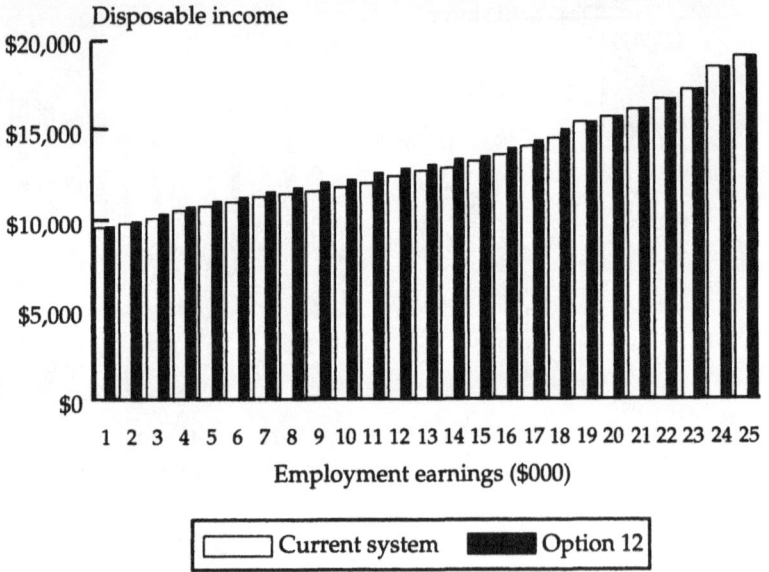

Disposable income

Caledon Institute of Social Policy

FIGURE 37
Marginal Tax Rate, Single Employable Person,
Option 12 – Low-Income Tax Credit/Lower Variable
Exemption to 67%

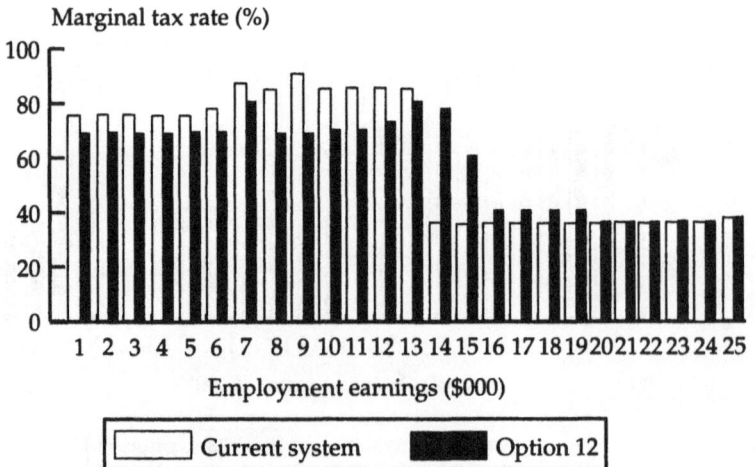

Marginal tax rate (%)

Caledon Institute of Social Policy

earnings exemption for welfare recipients of 67 per cent examined in Option 2. Option 12 extends the welfare threshold from $13,000 to $15,000.

The results in figure 36 show that disposable income rises for all households with earnings between $2,000 and $19,000. Households between $8,000 and $13,000 are the biggest winners in that they have the highest percentage increase (i.e., more than five per cent) in their disposable income; those at $13,000 get eight per cent more. The gains in disposable income decrease from $14,000 and above as the Ontario low-income tax credit declines.

The marginal tax rate is lower than the current system for households with earnings up to $12,000. Marginal tax rates are higher between earnings of $13,000 and $20,000 because of the impact of the 10 per cent reduction rate built into the low-income tax credit, which adds to their tax burden even while improving their disposable income. Again, changes in disposable income as well as marginal tax rates must be taken into account in assessing options for reform.

Families with Children

The preceding options were explored using single employable welfare recipients as the base household. The study conducted for the Ontario Fair Tax Commission modelled several options for selected families with children. Since most of the results were similar to those for single employable individuals, only a summary of the key findings is presented here.

Generally speaking, the results for single-parent families with one child age 2, one-earner couples with two children ages 3 and 5, and two-earner couples with two children ages 10 and 15 were similar to those for single employable recipients. Doubling the flat-rate exemption produced modest increases in disposable income – the gains declining above earnings of $5,000 – and modestly raised the earnings threshold where eligibility for some assistance from STEP ends. Lowering the earnings exemption from the present 75 per cent to 67 per cent resulted in small increases in disposable income that rise with earnings and also extended the welfare supplement further up the earnings scale. Doubling the Ontario sales tax credit created negligible increments in disposable income for families at all earnings levels.

The one point of noticeable difference between STEP families and single employable recipients concerned doubling the Ontario income tax reduction under Option 7. The Ontario income tax threshold for both one-parent families and two-parent households is considerably higher than it is for single employable recipients. Ontario income tax for single employable welfare recipients begins at earnings of just $9,000, which translates to an after-tax income $1,230 *below* the poverty line. By contrast, Ontario income tax starts at earnings of $19,000 or after-tax income $6,260 *above* the poverty line for single parents with one child age 2, earnings of $24,000 or after-tax income $2,901 above the poverty line for one-earner couples with two children ages 3 and 5, and earnings of $23,000 or after-tax income that is $2,292 above the poverty line for two-earner couples with two children ages 10 and 15.

As a result, options that reduce income taxes (e.g., doubling the Ontario tax reduction and introducing a low-income tax credit) are less relevant for families on STEP than for single employable recipients. Doubling the Ontario income tax reduction helps families with employment earnings higher up the scale (e.g., in the case of one-parent families, $20,000 to $30,000 in earnings) whose incomes are thousands of dollars above the poverty line. However, this conclusion does not mean that income tax relief is irrelevant to all lower-income families: many working poor families not on the STEP program get most of their income from paid work and have to pay income taxes.

We also experimented with a highly targeted federal child tax benefit option that substantially increased benefits for lower-income families. Using existing spending on the federal child tax benefit, we came up with an option that increased the maximum basic credit from $1,020 to $2,571 and retained the $213 supplement for children ages 6 and under. Such a hefty boost in the maximum benefit required lowering the net family income threshold from the present $25,921 to $18,000 and raising the reduction rate from the current 2.5 per cent for families with one child and 5 per cent for those with two or more children to 25 per cent.

This option jettisons the earned-income supplement component of the current federal child tax benefit, which discriminates against poor families on welfare or unemployment insurance, in favour of a much larger – two-and-a-half times – child benefit for all poor families with net incomes below $18,000, whatever the source of that income. Because of the much steeper reduction rate required to maximize benefits to lower-income families, the proposed child benefit would disappear at net incomes of $29,136 for families with one child age 6 and under, $40,272 for families with two children ages 6 and under, and $38,568 for families with two children ages 7 or older.

Finally, the analysis of the interface between the welfare and tax/

transfer systems explored the possibility of adapting a Quebec-style Parental Wage Assistance Program (Aide aux parents pour leurs revenus du travail, or APPORT) to Ontario. APPORT supplements the employment earnings of low-income families with children by providing an earnings supplement, a housing subsidy, and an amount to help offset child care costs. The results found that a wage supplement based on the APPORT parameters results in a significant increase in disposable income over a broad earnings range.

Income-in-Kind

This analysis of the interaction of the welfare and tax/transfer systems would not be complete without some discussion of income-in-kind. The latter refers to the benefits that the welfare system provides not as cash but as goods and services. Income-in-kind includes, for example, health-related benefits, dental care, medications, and assistance for work-related costs, such as clothing and transportation. We could not attribute a specific monetary value to these items because they vary enormously by household. Nonetheless, these can be worth significant amounts of money, especially for families that incur very high health-related costs.

Poor households with high health-related costs, in particular, are much better off on welfare than they are in the paid labour market. In making this observation, we are not suggesting that these benefits be taken away. If anything, it is worth exploring how it might be possible to extend similar health-related benefits to all low-income households and not simply to those "fortunate" enough to receive welfare.

Perhaps the key problem from the perspective of working parents is the availability of high-quality, affordable child care. It appears that welfare recipients have more ready access to subsidized child care than do working poor families (who may still qualify for subsidized care but often appear to receive less priority in terms of need). Again, the solution is not to reduce access for welfare recipients, but to improve access for working poor families so that the more ready availability of licensed subsidized care is not the factor that "ties" families to the welfare system.

Conclusion

There are numerous options for reducing the overall tax burden for welfare recipients who work. These options include changes to the welfare system, the federal income tax system, and the Ontario income tax system, and combinations of changes to these three systems.

The analysis of various options for reducing the tax burden on welfare recipients as they move into the labour market shows that most of the changes would generate only modest improvements in disposable income and would have a mixed impact on marginal tax rates, in some cases actually raising rather than lowering them. Yet these small improvements should not be dismissed, for two reasons. First, they would provide some additional and welcome funds to low-income families. Second, they represent feasible options in that they could be effected within the current tax/transfer system without major structural changes.

Larger increases to the disposable income of welfare recipients would require changing the welfare system itself. The welfare taxback represents, by far, the greatest proportion of the overall tax burden for welfare households. The greater the reduction in the welfare taxback, the more the increase in disposable income and (for most families) the larger the reduction in marginal tax rates; on the other hand, some families would face higher marginal tax rates because they now would qualify for welfare supplements.

However, options that focus solely upon improving the welfare system could create unintended and undesirable effects – such as making welfare a more attractive option for certain households than paid work and increasing welfare expenditures at a time when they already are extremely high. Such options also could have the effect of opening up the welfare net by raising the earnings threshold within which recipients still may qualify for assistance. Lowering the welfare taxback, then, could prove to be fiscally and politically problematic.

This problem can be addressed in several ways or through a combination of measures. First, to help reduce somewhat the costs of lowering the welfare taxback, welfare could be taxed in the same way as employment earnings, though there also should be a low-income tax credit available to all poor people. A second measure could involve the extension of income-in-kind to working poor families as well as welfare families. A major disincentive to leaving the welfare system thereby would be removed. Finally, a wage supplementation program similar to the Quebec model could help ensure that paid work is always a more attractive option than welfare.

Changes to the federal and Ontario income tax systems would have only a small impact upon disposable income and marginal tax rates. Nonetheless, raising the taxpaying threshold to the after-tax low-income cut-off by means of a fully indexed low-income tax credit would help remove a significant disincentive to full-time employment. Raising the taxpaying threshold to the poverty line also would help improve equity between welfare poor and working poor households because neither would pay income taxes. A low-income tax credit should be based on family rather than individual income and its threshold should vary by family size.

Increases to the GST and Ontario sales tax credits would have only a very slight impact on disposable income. By contrast, more generous low-income credits would have a larger – albeit still modest – impact on disposable income.

The three options intended for families with children would produce significant increases in disposable income. The targeted federal child tax benefit is two-and-a-half times larger than the current child tax benefit and produced gains in disposable income of up to 12 per cent for the families with two children. The two Quebec-derived wage supplementation options raised disposable income by almost 20 per cent.

The exploration of numerous options proved that it is important to examine more than marginal tax rates alone in gauging the viability of any proposals for reform. Changes in disposable income are equally, if not more, important in assessing which options are most appropriate and what their distributional consequences may be. So also, of course, are the relative costs of various options for change.

In short, there is no single "correct," simple, or cost-free solution to easing the onerous tax burden on welfare recipients who supplement their benefits by working in the labour force. The appropriate measures for reform can be determined only in relation to desired goals – reducing the tax burden for recipients at the bottom of the earnings scale, lowering the tax burden for households with higher earnings to help them move off welfare, introducing horizontal equity in the income tax treatment of the welfare poor and the working poor, or concentrating assistance on poor families with children.

Note

We would like to thank Allan Maslove for his comments and support throughout this project. We also gratefully acknowledge the assistance of David Mercer, Policy Development and Program Design, Ontario Ministry of Community and Social Services, and the comments of professor Allan

Moscovitch, Carleton University School of Social Work. The Centre for International Statistics, Canadian Council on Social Development, modelled our child benefit option using the Social Policy Simulation Database and Model (SPSD/M) from Statistics Canada.

Bibliography

Ontario Social Assistance Review Committee. 1988. *Transitions*. Toronto: Queen's Printer for Ontario
Wilson, Michael H. 1987. *The White Paper on Tax Reform 1987*. Ottawa: Department of Finance Canada

3 A Profile of High-Income Ontarians

BRIAN MURPHY, ROSS FINNIE, and
MICHAEL WOLFSON

Introduction

The distribution of income can be likened to a parade. First, imagine
that every member of society is somehow transformed so that their
height is proportional to their income. Next, suppose that all individuals are lined up in order of their "height," and they begin parading
past. The parade actually starts with people whose heads are under-
ground – for example, self-employed business people who have suf-
fered net income losses. Then there is a long period when people can
barely be seen over the hood of a car, and it is well past the halfway
mark of the parade when we encounter people of average height. At
this point heights are beginning to increase quite dramatically. Finally,
in the last fraction of the parade there are a few individuals who are
so tall their heads cannot even be seen up in the clouds.

This vivid metaphor by Jan Pen (1971) conveys an accurate impres-
sion of Canada's distribution of income. Most data and analysis, however, cover only the beginning and middle of this parade. Concerns
about the extent of "poverty" (most often defined as low income) and
the character of Canada's social safety net invariably focus on the first
quarter or fifth of the parade. Similarly, discussion about the burdens
of income and sales taxes, or the phenomenon of the "disappearing
middle class," focus on the middle of the parade. By comparison, the
"giants" at the end of the parade have gone largely unstudied. This
paper provides a profile of these high-income Canadians, focusing
specifically on Ontario.

The study of high-income individuals touches important social and economic policy issues. Judgments regarding the equity of the tax and transfer system depend on the nature and extent of the redistribution of income. Continuing deficits by federal and provincial levels of government raise questions regarding the amount of revenue potentially obtainable from the "rich" and well-off. High effective tax rates often give rise to concerns about adverse incentives for a very dynamic part of the population and the subsequent impacts on the economy. Low effective tax rates, on the other hand, raise questions about whether so-called tax "loopholes" (more properly, "tax expenditures") are being properly used or appropriately targeted.

The plan of the paper is as follows. First, we address the issue of defining high income – when does a "tall" person become a "giant"? Next, we proceed to draw a profile of high-income Ontarians in terms of their characteristics and patterns of income and taxes. Third, we examine the patterns of income over time – how stable are the incomes of "rich" Ontarians?

Defining High Income

Deciding who are the "rich" in Canada has not been a widely debated topic in parliamentary committees, the popular press, or scholarly publications. For some observers, "rich" people live on palatial estates in exotic locations, own fleets of cars, stables of horses, and so forth. To others – perhaps the homeless or governments in need of tax revenues – someone with high income could mean just a comfortable, middle-class person. An appropriate dividing line obviously falls between these two extremes – but where precisely do we draw the line? The following discussion provides some background to the choice of a definition of high income that will be used in this analysis.

Drawing Low- and Middle-Income Lines

A number of recent works have focused on defining families with *low* incomes (Ruggles 1990, Wolfson and Evans 1990). The debate on the definition of poverty has advocates for both an absolute and relative definition. An absolute approach to determining a low-income line estimates the income required to purchase minimum amounts of food (in terms of calories per day), shelter (as minimum rental rates), clothing, and other basic household expenditures. The Montreal Diet Dispensary guidelines are an example of such lines.[1] The relative approach, on the other hand, claims that low income is relative to the well-being of all members of society. The Canadian Council on Social Development, for example, uses a relative definition of 50 per cent of average family income.

Once calculated, these lines must be updated from year to year. There is both an absolute and relative way in which this can be done. Absolute updating inflates lines using price indexes. The official U.S. poverty line is an example of this absolute updating. Relative lines would be updated using such statistics as the growth in median income. Statistics Canada's Low Income Measure is an example of such updating. To the extent that the growth in, for example, median income outpaces inflation, relative updating will produce higher cut-offs over time than will absolute updating.

Many studies (OECD 1982, Wolfson and Evans 1990) use the relative definitions of poverty or low income, with the most widely used definition being 50 per cent of median income (Buhman et al. 1988, Statistics Canada 1991). Similarly, the middle class is defined as those individuals having between x per cent and y per cent of the median income. One definition sets x at 75 per cent and y at 150 per cent (Wolfson 1989, 1993). Intuitively, the relative approach is most appealing with regards to high incomes and is consistent with most of the Canadian low-income lines and international comparisons.

The "Greenbook" Database

Before we look at the distribution of incomes of Canada and Ontario, we will describe the data that we will be using in the main part of this paper. The first part of this analysis uses the 1990 "Greenbook" microdata file, which forms the basis of the annual publication *Taxation Statistics*, commonly known as the "Greenbook" (Revenue Canada 1992). For 1990, the Greenbook file is a two per cent sample of 17.6 million Canadian tax filers, and includes detailed income and tax information on 355,622 tax filers. For Ontario the overall sample size is 110,000, representing 6.65 million filers. The sample is particularly suited for this study as it is stratified to capture particularly sparse groups of the population, such as high-income filers. Thus the sample includes all filers with incomes over $450,000 (approximately the top 0.1 per cent) and about 50 per cent of all filers with incomes between $350,000 and $450,000.

The Greenbook file is very different from the survey databases commonly used to study low and middle incomes. The Greenbook does not include all individuals in Canada – only individuals who file tax returns. Moreover, the Greenbook does not include in its definition of income several government transfer payments. However, given the income-tested nature of these transfer programs, high-income individuals receive an insignificant portion of these transfers, and these make up only a tiny fraction of the incomes of high-income filers. The Greenbook reports the taxable amounts of capital gains and dividend income. In this analysis we have adjusted these amounts to represent the actual income received from these sources.

The Greenbook represents individuals, not families (though family data have been constructed from tax returns – such as the LAD discussed below). To the extent that high-income families may use various forms of income splitting, the data used here will understate the upper tail of the income distribution.

The Distribution of Income in Canada and Ontario

Tables 1 and 2 give a sense of the overall distribution of individual income tax filers in Canada and Ontario.[2] Table 1 presents the income percentiles for Canada and Ontario. The first two columns show the incomes at a variety of percentile thresholds. Over one-half of all *Canadian tax filers* have incomes below $20,000 (this is quite different from the more familiar Statistics Canada Survey of Consumer Finances [SCF] data on families, because of differences in coverage and the treatment of multiple-income families).[3] Over 80 per cent of individuals have incomes below two times median (i.e., $40,000), and about 95 per cent are below three times median (i.e., $60,000).

If we compare Ontario with Canada as a whole, Ontario filers have higher incomes throughout virtually the entire distribution. The size of the Canada–Ontario difference is greater at higher income levels, reaching $17,000 at the 99th percentile. Thus the highest incomes in Ontario are higher than those in other provinces. The last two columns offer another perspective by showing the percentile thresholds as a per cent of median income in Canada and Ontario respectively.

For a clearer picture of the distribution of incomes of individual tax filers in Canada and Ontario, table 2 shows the average incomes and income shares for various percentile *groups*. The boxed area in the middle shows statistics for income quintiles, while the rows above and below describe the tails of the distribution. The distribution is more unequal than the distribution for families (not shown). For example, the Statistics Canada Survey of Consumer Finances (SCF) reports that for all families and unattached individuals in 1990 43.3 per cent of total

TABLE 1
Individual Total Income Percentiles, Canada and Ontario, 1990

Percentile	Percentile Threshold ($000s)		Percentile Threshold as a Percent of Median Income	
	Canada	Ontario	Canada	Ontario
1	0.1	0.1	1	1
5	1.1	1.5	5	7
10	3.7	4.4	19	20
20	7.6	8.5	39	39
25	9.4	10.6	48	48
40	15.3	17.3	77	78
50	19.8	22.0	100	100
60	24.6	27.2	125	123
75	33.7	36.3	171	165
80	37.7	40.4	191	184
90	49.4	53.1	250	241
95	61.4	65.8	311	299
99	114.1	131.5	578	597

Source: Special tabulations, 1990 Greenbook file (Revenue Canada 1992)
Note: Total income as measured using tax data excludes GIS, Social Assistance, Workers' Compensation, and some other government transfers, but includes OAS and CPP/QPP. For this study the refundable sales tax credit and refundable child tax credit have been included in total income. Capital gains and dividends are actual amounts received, not taxable amounts.

income went to the top quintile, while 4.7 per cent went to the bottom quintile. For individual tax filers the comparable shares were 49 per cent and 3 per cent respectively. The basis of this study is, however, *tax filing* individuals, and tax filers are somewhat more unequally distributed partly because they do not have to report various transfer payments.

As in table 1, average incomes for Ontarians are higher than Canadian averages in all groups, with the exception of those groups reporting average losses.[4] The figures in the second pair of columns in table 2 show that while incomes in Ontario are higher, income shares are virtually identical for Canada and Ontario, with only the top one per cent in Ontario receiving a slightly larger share.

Drawing a High-Income Line

With this perspective on the general shape of the income distribution, we now move toward a working definition of "high income." A num-

TABLE 2
Average Income and Income Share by Percentile Income Group, Canada
and Ontario, 1990

Percentile group	Mean[a]		Income Share	
	Canada	Ontario	Canada	Ontario
Bottom 1	–4	–6.2	0%	0%
Bottom 5	–0.4	–0.7	0%	0%
Bottom 10	0.9	1.1	0%	0%
Bottom 20	3.3	3.8	3%	3%
20–40	10.8	12.2	9%	9%
40–60	19.8	22.1	16%	16%
60–80	30.6	33.2	24%	24%
Top 20	62	69	49%	49%
Top 10	75.6	85.1	36%	36%
Top 5	107.7	125.1	24%	24%
Top 1	231.6	287.1	9%	10%

Source: Special tabulations, 1990 Greenbook file (Revenue Canada 1992)
[a] Means are rounded to the nearest $100.

ber of studies have, in fact, already drawn a line for high-income
groups. The U.S. Bureau of the Census (1987) conducted a study to
provide marketers with a guide for identifying populations with discretionary income (income remaining after day-to-day needs are met).
The definition of "having discretionary income" was arbitrarily set at
a point where households have disposable incomes 30 per cent higher
than the average disposable income (within various size, age, and
location groups). This is obviously a relative definition. The study
found (coincidentally) that 30 per cent of American households have
discretionary income. By referring to table 1 above, we see that this
would translate into a line of about $35,000 for Ontario – arguably too
low for a high-income line.

In another U.S. study, Danzinger, Gottschalk, and Smolensky (1989)
defined the "rich" as persons living in families with family incomes
exceeding nine times the U.S. poverty line. This produced a line of
about $95,000 in 1987 current dollars and resulted in an incidence of
high-income persons of seven per cent. If we were to use a similar
seven per cent incidence, the data for Ontario in table 1 would produce
a high-income threshold of about $60,000, albeit for individuals rather
than families.

Of course, these U.S. lines do not strictly apply to Canada. The distribution of income here is more equal (Wolfson and Murphy 1992), so there are fewer giants in our parade, and compared with those in the United States they are not as tall. For example, from data from the SCF and the U.S. Current Population Survey, 2.8 per cent of U.S. families had incomes above three times the median family income, which is twice that in Canada.[5] Also the average income for the top five per cent of families in the United States was $137,000, compared with $120,000 in Canada (Wolfson and Murphy 1992).[6]

A quite different approach to the definition of high income is to infer it from federal and provincial surtax structures. A surtax is an additional tax calculated as a percentage of basic federal or provincial tax. In the case of a *high-income* surtax, the additional tax begins only when basic taxes exceed a given threshold. In 1990, the federal high-income surtax started at $15,000 of basic federal tax. An individual filer would require a minimum taxable income of $70,000 to face a $15,000 tax liability, so $70,000 could be taken as an implicit "high-income line."[7]

The tax system can, and has, shifted this implicit "definition" of high income quite often. By 1993 a taxable income of $62,260 would have been sufficient to trigger the high-income surtax – an 11 per cent drop over three years. Similarly, in Ontario, this implicit definition of high income was $83,300 in 1990 and by 1993 had dropped 17 per cent to $69,200.

In this context, and as a somewhat arbitrary definition, we will be using a relative definition of high income – roughly three times median income – which results in a high-income threshold of $66,000 for Ontario in 1990. For ease of calculation and consistency in tables, we have used as a working definition the cut-point for the top five per cent of Ontarians: a threshold of $65,800.

Let us now place this definition into the context of the distribution of income in Ontario. The top chart of figure 1 shows the distribution of income for all Ontario tax filers. The bottom chart gives an expanded view of the top five per cent of Ontarians – those with incomes exceeding the three times median income definition (i.e., the right-most bar of the top chart). This chart illustrates our parade metaphor: The horizontal axis in the top chart divides the tax filing population into 20 groups of equal size. The vertical axis then shows the mean income of each 1/20th group relative to the mean income of all filers. For example, the richest five per cent of filers had in excess of four times the mean income. As the bottom chart shows, the top 0.25 per cent of filers had incomes that average over 20 times the average for all filers.

FIGURE 1
Relative Mean Incomes by Percentile Group, All Tax Filers
and Top 5 Per Cent of Filers, Ontario 1990

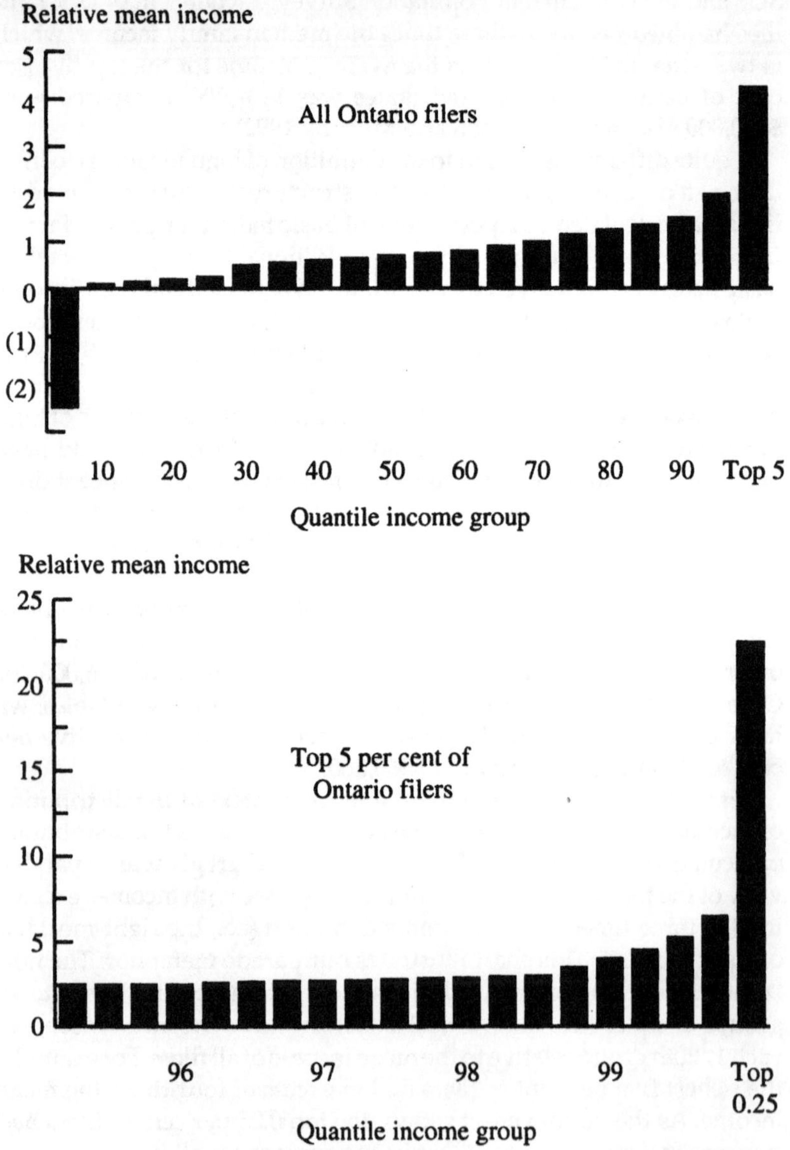

Source: Special tabulations, 1990 Greenbook file (Revenue Canada 1992)

Ontario Tax Filers in 1990

We turn now to a profile of high-income Ontarians using the 1990 Greenbook file. This section is organized into three parts. The first part compares the distribution and average incomes of high-income filers with non–high-income filers by age, sex, marital status, and occupation. The next part examines tax rates. The third part looks at the income and tax profiles of Ontarians.

Demographic Profiles

Table 3 looks at filers across three dimensions: sex, marital status, and age. The column structure is repeated throughout much of the analysis and warrants some explanation here. The table is divided into two groups of four columns each; one group shows the percentage distribution of filers and the other group their average incomes. The four columns within each group show four different segments of filers – labelled Quintile Income Group. The first two columns split the population at the 95th percentile. The lower-income 95 per cent of filers are in the first of these columns, and the top 5 per cent of filers in the second. Together these two columns include all filers. The next two columns show progressively better-off subsets of the top five per cent of filers – first the top one per cent and then the top tenth of one per cent. The rows of table 3 show the three characteristics of interest – sex, marital status, and age. The percentages within each of these breakdowns sum vertically to 100. So, for example, individual filers aged 25–44 represent 46.6 per cent of the bottom 95 per cent of tax filers in 1990 and 40.6 per cent of the top 5 per cent. The first row of the Percent Population group gives the estimated population in thousands. The second set of four columns presents average incomes.

In general, high-income filers tend to be middle-aged, married, and male. Figures in table 3 show that males dominate the high-income tax filing population, peaking at 87.2 per cent of the top 0.1 per cent. Married filers also dominate the high-income group, representing 77.6 per cent of those filers. Younger individuals are relatively rare among the top 5 per cent, which is dominated by those over age 44. Similarly, average incomes increase with age among the top 5 per cent. The average incomes among high-income males, elderly (and the 45–64 group), and married filers are the highest of their respective sex, age, and marital status groups, over $125 thousand in each case.

Table 4 has the same structure as table 3 but presents tax filers by

TABLE 3
Distribution and Mean Incomes of Individual Tax Filers by Income Group, Age, Sex, and Marital Status, Ontario, 1990

	Per Cent Population by Quantile Income Group				Average Income ($000s) by Quantile Income Group			
	0–95	Top 5	Top 1	Top 0.1	0–95	Top 5	Top 1	Top 0.1
All (000s)	6,318	332.4	66.5	6.6	23	125	286	1,002
Sex								
Male	49.5	80.6	85.0	87.2	27	128	291	1,025
Female	50.5	19.4	15.0	12.8	19	112	261	840
Marital status								
Single	46.4	22.4	16.8	16.6	19	114	279	958
Married	53.6	77.6	83.2	83.4	26	128	288	1,010
Age								
0–24	15.1	0.4	0.5	0.5	12	129	265	844
25–44	46.6	40.6	35.6	24.5	26	112	251	927
45–64	24.2	46.9	49.0	56.2	27	131	304	1,027
65 +	14.1	12.0	15.0	18.9	20	144	315	1,028

Source: Special tabulations, 1990 Greenbook file (Revenue Canada 1992)

occupation. Business employees dominate every income group and comprise 52.9 per cent of the top 0.1 per cent group (about 3,500 individuals), where they are likely to be top executives. Government employees are the second-largest group both below and above the 95th percentile; however, few remain above the 99th percentile. Other occupations that have lower representation among the higher-income segments of the population include farmers/fishermen, pensioners, and others. There are virtually no professionals in the non–high-income group, while they make up a significant share of the top one per cent of filers. Investors are also more concentrated among the higher percentile groups. Investors show a fourfold increase in proportional representation, rising from 6.6 per cent of the 0–95 group to 31.0 per cent of the top 0.1 group, second only to top business employees.

To lead us into the section on taxes, figure 2 presents the percentage shares of income and taxes for the four income groups. The shares are calculated as the ratio of total income or taxes for each income group to total income or taxes for all Ontarians. Total tax includes federal plus provincial taxes, including the repayment of OAS and Family Allowances, plus payroll taxes. Total income is income as reported in the Greenbook using *total* capital gains and dividend income plus the child tax credit and sales tax credit.[8] The bottom 95 per cent of the tax filer population receives 77.8 per cent of the income and pays 69.2 per

TABLE 4
Distribution and Mean Incomes of Individual Tax Filers by Occupational Group,
Ontario, 1990[a]

	Percent Population by Quantile Income Group				Average Income ($000s) by Quantile Income Group			
	0–95	Top 5	Top 1	Top 0.1	0–95	Top 5	Top 1	Top 0.1
Business employee	50.9	48.3	42.7	52.9	25	124	313	1,080
Government[b]	16.3	19.7	3.2	–	32	83	165	–
Farmers/fishermen	0.8	0.4	0.2	–	17	107	283	–
Accountants	0.0	0.6	0.9	–	31	127	195	–
Doctors, dentists	0.1	4.9	14.0	4.1	37	165	214	593
Notaries, lawyers	0.1	1.7	4.2	2.4	34	165	234	682
Other professional	0.7	1.8	2.2	2.3	22	139	290	999
Investors	6.6	15.4	26.0	31.0	21	165	305	917
Property owners	0.8	1.0	1.8	1.4	15	149	246	884
Pensioners	12.5	2.8	0.9	–	18	87	196	–
Others	11.3	3.5	3.9	5.1	10	144	349	1,239
All	100.0	100.0	100.0	100.0	23	125	286	1,002

Source: Special tabulations, 1990 Greenbook file (Revenue Canada 1992)
[a] Self-reported occupation from income tax returns.
[b] Government includes federal/provincial/municipal employees, teachers, institutions, and Crown corporations.
– Sample size less than 25. If the sample size of a particular cell in any of the tables is below 25 then the information for that cell is suppressed.

cent of the taxes, while the top 5 per cent of tax filers receive the remaining 22.2 per cent of all income and pay 30.8 per cent of all taxes. Note that the ratio of taxes to total income steadily rises with higher-income groups.

Effective Tax Rates

Tax rates are an important indicator of the fairness of a tax system. Tax rates in relation to income are a good measure of the vertical equity of a system whose basic principle is taxation according to the ability to pay. This principle is generally interpreted to mean that those with higher incomes should face higher tax rates. However, the tax system is not only used as a tool for achieving vertical equity; fairness, or equity, also means that people in similar circumstances should be taxed in a similar way (horizontal equity). The tax system is also asked to meet other goals, such as simplicity, efficiency, revenue generation,

FIGURE 2

Distribution of Income and Taxes by Quantile Income Group, Ontario, 1990

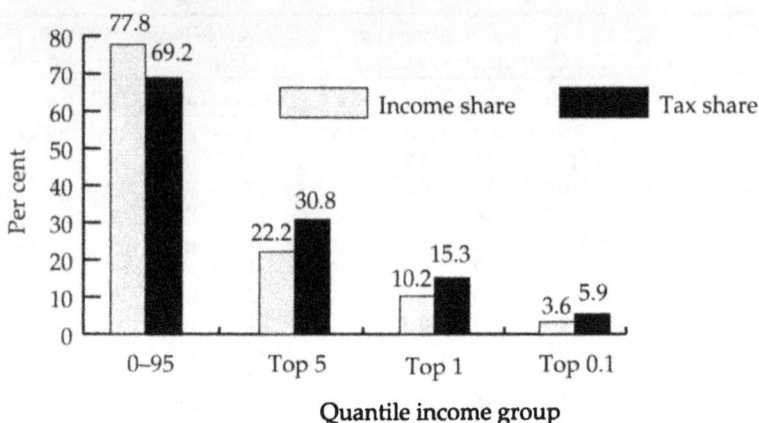

Source: Special tabulations, 1990 Greenbook file (Revenue Canada 1992)

and the granting of various concessions and incentives referred to as tax expenditures. These goals are often competing and the political process determines the appropriate balance.

There are a number of different tax rates that can be examined. *Nominal* tax rates are the rates provided in legislation. The statutory federal personal income tax rates of .17, .26, and .29 are one example. A *marginal* tax rate is the rate at which additional income would be taxed (i.e., how much tax is payable on an additional dollar of income). These rates are sensitive to the kind of additional income and the unit of analysis (i.e., individual or family), as we shall see later. Effective tax rates are what we will be focusing on in this analysis. They are calculated as the ratio of the taxes paid to the total income of an individual or group.

The general progressivity of the personal income tax system, roughly indicated by figure 2 above, is shown more directly in figure 3 below. There are five sets of bars, one set for each quantile income group, and one set for all filers. The height of the bars represents the effective tax rate or ETR (the proportion of total income paid in taxes). Tax rates are clearly higher in the higher-income groups. The set of two bars shows two different ways in which ETRs may be calculated, and, as can be seen, the results are somewhat different. The first of the two bars is calculated using the more common approach of dividing *total taxes*

FIGURE 3
Effective Tax Rates by Quantile Income Group, Ontario, 1990

ETR

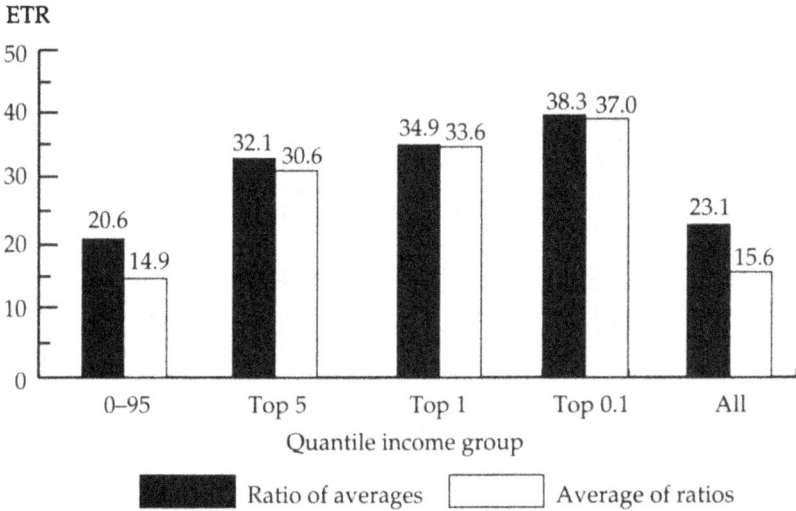

Quantile income group

■ Ratio of averages   □ Average of ratios

Source: Special tabulations, 1990 Greenbook file (Revenue Canada 1992)

paid by all filers in the group by their corresponding *total income*. Thus, according to this method, 20.6 per cent of all income for the non–high-income population is paid out in taxes. The second bar is calculated by first computing each individual filer's ratio of taxes to total income, and then averaging these individual ETRs. This gives the average ETR across individuals and results in lower effective tax rates. For example, non–high-income tax filers paid 14.9 per cent of their income to taxes. The key difference is that in the first case the effective tax rate is weighted by income, and in the second case by population. We shall use the latter method in the rest of the analysis. Either way, however, figure 3 shows a generally progressive structure of effective federal plus Ontario tax rates. From 14.9 per cent, the rates climb to 30.6 per cent, 33.6 per cent, and finally, 37.0 per cent.

The ETRs in figure 3 may still seem low, averaging well under 20 per cent overall and about 30 per cent for the top five group, especially when compared with the statutory tax rate of 50.2 per cent for Ontario residents in 1990. It is critical, however, to keep in mind the difference between average and marginal tax rates.

In order to highlight the distinction between marginal and average rates, figure 4 compares average effective tax rates with two types of

114   Brian Murphy, Ross Finnie, and Michael Wolfson

FIGURE 4
Simulated Tax Rates by Year for the Top 5 Per cent of Filers and
the Bottom 95 Per cent of Filers, Ontario, 1988

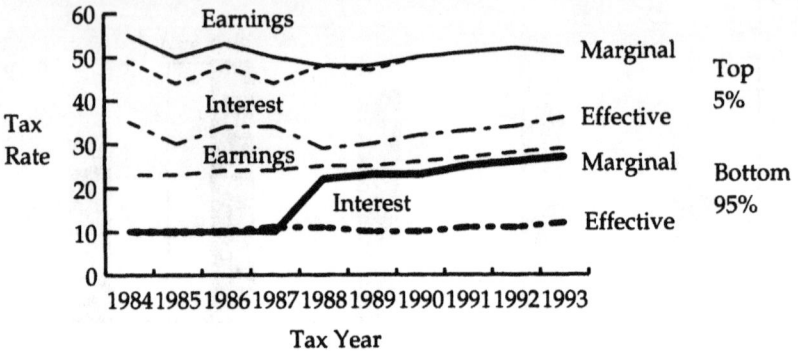

Source: Special tabulations using SPSD/M Version 5.1

marginal rates using the Social Policy Simulation Database and Model
(SPSD/M) (Bordt et al. 1990). The tax and transfer system rules, rates,
and levels from each of the 10 years 1984 to 1993 were applied to a
1988 population of individual tax filers, and the results were split into
two income groups: the bottom 95 per cent and the top 5 per cent. Also,
because the tax treatment of earnings and interest has differed significantly, marginal rates for each income source have been estimated.
The simulated average effective tax rates (labelled "Effective" in the
graph) are at roughly the same levels as calculated using the Greenbook
file. They have been generally increasing over the past decade for the
tax filer population as a whole. In particular, there has been more
fluctuation in the high-income population due to numerous changes
to top federal tax brackets and to high-income surtaxes. The "marginal" tax rates, in contrast, have been estimated by simulating the
incremental tax liability each individual would have faced if either
their earnings or interest income had been increased by a small amount.
The resulting marginal tax rates were then averaged across all filers
within each income group. They are consistently at least 15 per cent
higher than the effective rates.[9]

    Table 5 shows ETRs by demographic group. Male filers have slightly
higher tax rates than females, as do married couples relative to single
persons. This is due to their higher average incomes. The elderly have
among the lowest ETRs – below 10 per cent – in the non–high-income
group, and among the highest ETRs in the high-income groups. These

TABLE 5
Mean Effective Tax Rates of All Individuals by Age, Sex, and Marital Status,
Ontario, 1990

| | Effective Tax Rate Quantile Income Group | | | |
	0–95	Top 5	Top 1	Top 0.1
All	14.9	30.6	33.6	37.0
Sex				
Male	17.1	31.0	34.1	37.3
Female	12.7	28.8	31.0	34.3
Marital Status				
Single	12.9	29.7	31.6	35.1
Married	16.6	30.8	34.0	37.3
Age				
0–24	10.0	28.1	30.9	26.6
25–44	17.4	31.0	34.3	37.1
45–64	17.0	30.4	33.4	36.9
65 +	8.2	29.8	32.8	37.0

Source: Special tabulations, 1990 Greenbook file (Revenue Canada 1992)

results are also consistent with the table 3 figures on average incomes. However, 25–44-year-old filers have lower average incomes than the 45–65-year-old filers but experience higher ETRs in the high-income groups. This is likely an income composition effect, where younger high-income earners do not have as high a proportion of incomes from investments as do their slightly older counterparts.

Table 6 presents average effective tax rates by occupation. The lowest marginal rates in all high-income groups are experienced by investors; 24.2 per cent in the high-income group, 6.4 per cent below average for that group. This is likely due to the more favourable tax treatment accorded investment income in comparison to labour income. Thus the recipients of labour income – business employees and certain professionals – experience the highest rates.

As a reflection of the general progressivity of the tax system, within the non–high-income population, occupations with above-average ETRs are the same occupations that had above-average incomes (see table 4). However, for the high-income filers, accountants, investors, and others have above-average incomes and below-average ETRs. This relationship was true of only investors in the top one per cent and investors and property owners in the top 0.1 per cent. Again, this is likely due to the more favourable tax treatment accorded investment income in comparison to labour income.

The effective tax rates by occupation show more variability across

TABLE 6
Effective Tax Rates of All Individuals by Occupation and Quantile Income Group,
Ontario, 1990

| Occupation | Effective Tax Rate Quantile Income Group | | | |
	0–95	Top 5	Top 1	Top 0.1
Business employee	17.5	32.1	37.5	41.5
Government	20.2	31.1	36.0	–
Farm/fish	9.4	25.6	23.6	–
Accountants	15.1	30.2	32.9	–
Doctors, dentists	20.7	33.8	36.4	40.1
Notaries, lawyers	19.7	33.8	36.5	40.0
Other professional	13.6	32.0	36.3	40.9
Investors	11.7	24.2	24.9	27.7
Property owners	10.8	28.5	33.3	35.7
Pensioners	7.2	29.2	35.2	–
Others	6.4	30.1	33.5	40.5
All	14.9	30.6	33.6	37.0

Source: Special tabulations, 1990 Greenbook file (Revenue Canada 1992)
– Sample size less than 25

occupations than across the various demographic breakdowns.[10] Another important source of variation in ETRs is differential access to and/or use of various deductions and tax credits. Through use of such tax provisions, 225 filers of the top 0.1 per cent of filers had effective tax rates of 10 per cent or lower; some 75 filers had reduced their ETRs to one per cent or lower.[11] While this phenomenon is most striking at high levels of income, there are individual tax filers at all income levels who experience these low rates.

Figure 5 below highlights the relationship between income and ETRs. The bars indicate the proportion of filers with ETRs of 10 per cent or lower ("low" ETRs) by percentile income group across the horizontal axis, and the solid line gives average ETRs. The width of each bar is proportional to the size of the population it represents. As was implied by figures given earlier, average ETRs rise steadily with income at all income levels. Virtually all filers in the first two decile groups have ETRs below 10 per cent. The proportion drops quickly over the next seven decile groups, with 1.6 per cent of filers in the ninth decile having "low ETRs." The final three bars represent the 90th–95th, 96th–99th, and the top percentile. While the ETRs continue to increase for these groups, the percentage with "low ETRs" actually increases

FIGURE 5
Proportion of Filers with ETRs of 10 Per Cent or Lower
and Average ETR by Percentile Group, Ontario, 1990

Per cent

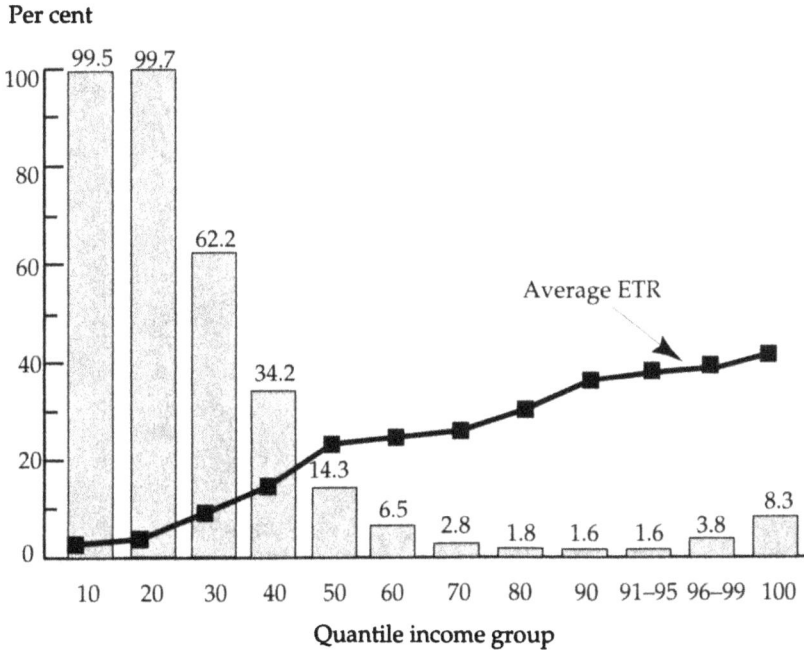

Quantile income group

Source: Special tabulations, 1990 Greenbook file (Revenue Canada 1992)

as well. The top percentile group have a greater proportion of filers
with "low ETRs" than do filers in all decile groups above the median.

Income and Tax Profiles

We now turn to examine the composition of income and the use of
deductions and tax credits. Table 7 has two sets of four columns. The
first set presents the share of total income by income source. So, for
example, 74.5 per cent of total income in the 0–95th percentile group
was employment income (wages, commissions, and gratuities). The
second set of columns gives the per cent of filers reporting income from
each particular source.

Wages and salaries form the majority of total income in all four

TABLE 7
Per Cent Shares of Total Income by Source and Per Cent of Filers Reporting Different
Types of Income by Quantile Income Group, Ontario, 1990

	Per Cent Share of Total Income Quantile Income Group				Per Cent of Filers Reporting Quantile Income Group			
	0–95	Top 5	Top 1	Top 0.1	0–95	Top 5	Top 1	Top 0.1
Employment								
Subtotal	74.5	58.6	47.7	54.3	73.0	80.0	69.1	82.5
Investment								
Interest	7.4	9.9	10.5	10.9	53.9	84.2	90.9	96.4
Partnership	−0.1	−0.5	−0.7	−0.9	0.4	8.7	22.1	31.9
Dividends	0.7	5.1	7.4	9.5	7.9	38.0	52.1	65.8
Capital gains	0.6	8.2	12.2	11.9	2.7	20.8	36.1	45.0
Other	4.2	3.0	1.9	1.3	18.2	29.4	33.2	38.3
Subtotal	12.9	25.8	31.4	32.7	58.8	90.2	95.2	98.9
Self-employment								
Business	1.3	1.2	1.3	2.2	6.1	6.6	7.5	13.5
Professional	0.8	10.5	15.5	6.0	1.4	13.5	26.2	14.5
Other	0.3	0.5	0.3	0.2	2.1	3.7	5.5	4.9
Subtotal	2.5	12.1	17.2	8.4	9.4	22.4	35.8	29.7
Transfers	8.7	1.2	0.6	0.2	65.3	54.3	58.3	53.7
Alimony & other	1.4	2.4	3.1	4.4	12.3	22.3	32.0	34.4
Total	100.0	100.0	100.0	100.0	99.9	100.0	100.0	100.0
Multiple income sources								
Employment *or* self-employment and investment					39.7	74.8	76.8	84.7
Employment *and* self-employment and investment					1.3	6.1	9.0	10.9

Source: Special tabulations, 1990 Greenbook file (Revenue Canada 1992)

income groups, but are more predominant among the first 95 per cent,
where this source makes up 74.5 per cent of income. Self-employment
income shows the most dramatic relative increase in importance – from
2.5 per cent for the non–high-income population to 12.1 per cent for
high incomes and 17.2 per cent for the top one per cent. Professional
income forms the lion's share of self-employment income but does
decline somewhat in importance at the highest incomes. Business
income on the other hand, while much smaller in absolute share,
increases in importance for the top tenth of one per cent of filers. Not
surprisingly, investment income also shows an increased importance
for high-income filers. While dividends and capital gains are a rela-

tively small 10 per cent of investment income for non–high-income filers, they form 65 per cent of investment income for the top 0.1 per cent of filers.

The second part of the table, which reports the percentage of tax filers reporting income from the various sources, supports the percentage share numbers. The dip in the reporting of employment income for the top one per cent is offset by the increase in self-employment income. A key feature is that it points to the underlying trend of higher-income groups more often reporting multiple sources of income. This point is made directly in the bottom portion of the table. The percentage of filers simultaneously reporting employment, self-employment, and investment income rose from 1.3 per cent of the non–high-income group to 10.9 per cent of the top 0.1 group.

In table 8 we present estimates similar to those in table 7, but for allowable deductions from income and for tax credits. The pattern of more filers reporting investment income in higher-income groups, and investment income accounting for a greater proportion of total income among those with higher incomes, is reflected in the use of deductions[12] and credits. Carrying charges, capital gains exemptions and exclusions, and the dividend tax credit show large increases for the high-income groups. The RPP, RRSP, and Other deductions and the personal nonrefundable credits form the overwhelming bulk of "write-offs" for the non–high-income population, and are only a small percentage of deductions and credits for high-income Ontarians.

Table 9 presents the share of income, deduction, and tax credits disaggregated by sex. In the income shares section of the table we see that a significantly higher proportion of females' total income comes from investment and other income, while a lower proportion comes from employment and unemployment earnings. More striking is the increase in the investment shares across income groups. Men's investment income as a share of total income rises two-and-one-half times between the non–high-income group and the top 0.1 group, while the women's share more than quadruples. This income pattern is similar for the capital gains deduction and the dividend tax credit. Carrying charges, however, are a fairly even proportion of deductions for high-income females, while they do increase for males. Overall these trends suggest that investment income is being split between high-income spouses (recall the high proportion of married filers in the high-income population).

TABLE 8
Per Cent Share of Deductions and Tax Credits and Per Cent of Filers Reporting by
Quantile Income Group, Ontario, 1990

	Per Cent Share Quantile Income Group				Per Cent Reporting Quantile Income Group			
	0–95	Top 5	Top 1	Top 0.1	0–95	Top 5	Top 1	Top 0.1
Deductions								
RPP	22.0	7.4	1.3	0.3	18.3	31.4	12.4	7.1
RRSP	38.4	22.1	14.3	6.0	22.0	58.5	68.2	69.4
Carrying charges	6.1	18.9	25.7	37.9	16.0	53.0	60.4	69.6
Capital gains exemption	6.3	34.4	43.2	42.8	2.0	14.5	22.6	26.0
Capital gains exclusion	2.7	16.7	22.6	29.9	2.7	20.8	36.1	45.0
Dividend gross up	−3.0	−10.3	−13.7	−23.7	7.9	38.0	52.1	65.8
Other	27.5	10.7	6.7	6.9	32.0	41.6	29.6	25.6
Total	100.0	100.0	100.0	100.0	56.2	96.0	97.2	97.5
Tax credits								
Charity & gifts	2.5	13.1	17.4	21.1	31.1	72.1	76.6	78.0
Federal political	0.0	0.1	0.1	0.1	0.5	3.2	5.6	8.6
Investment credit	0.0	0.2	0.5	0.6	0.0	0.1	0.4	0.4
Dividend credit	1.7	34.0	55.7	70.7	7.1	37.1	50.4	64.0
Personal & other credits	95.7	52.6	26.2	7.5	100.0	100.0	100.0	100.0
Total	100.0	100.0	100.0	100.0	100.0	100.0	100.0	100.0

Source: Special tabulations, 1990 Greenbook file (Revenue Canada 1992)

Ontario Tax Filers in 1990: Summary

High-income filers in Ontario tend to be middle-aged, married men.
Business and government employees make up about two-thirds of both
high- and non–high-income groups. The proportion of investors more
than doubles between the non–high- and high-income groups. In the
top 0.1 per cent income group, business employees account for more
than one-half of tax filers, and investors make up another 31 per cent.

The general progressivity of the tax system gives rise to the finding
that non–high-income tax filers receive about 80 per cent of all income
and pay about 70 per cent of federal and provincial income and payroll
taxes. The high-income filers receive the remaining 22 per cent of all
income and pay the balance of 31 per cent of the taxes. Effective tax
rates experienced by high-income filers are close to three times those
of non–high-income filers.

TABLE 9
Per Cent Share of Total Income by Quantile Income Group and Sex, Ontario, 1990

	Males				Females			
	0–95	Top 5	Top 1	Top 0.1	0–95	Top 5	Top 1	Top 0.1
Income source								
Employment	76.9	62.2	51.1	57.4	71.2	41.6	26.4	28.3
Investment	11.3	21.6	27.1	29.2	15.1	45.4	58.3	62.0
Self-employment	2.9	13.1	18.4	8.9	1.9	7.7	9.7	4.4
Transfers	7.9	1.0	0.5	0.2	9.9	2.0	1.0	0.3
Other	1.0	2.2	2.9	4.3	2.0	3.3	4.5	5.0
Total	100.0	100.0	100.0	100.0	100.0	100.0	100.0	100.0
Deductions								
RPP	21.5	7.9	1.5	0.3	22.7	5.8	0.6	0.1
RRSP	39.8	22.2	13.6	5.3	36.5	21.9	17.7	10.3
Carrying charges	7.2	21.2	28.7	41.5	4.6	10.7	11.4	12.9
Capital gains exemption	5.7	31.8	40.5	40.2	7.2	43.4	55.5	61.6
Capital gains exclusion	2.6	15.7	21.3	27.2	2.9	20.4	28.7	48.9
Dividend gross up	−2.6	−9.6	−12.6	−21.3	−3.6	−12.8	−18.9	−41.0
Other	25.9	10.8	7.1	6.8	29.7	10.5	4.9	7.2
Total	100.0	100.0	100.0	100.0	100.0	100.0	100.0	100.0
Tax Credits								
Charity & gifts	3.1	13.2	18.3	23.0	2.0	12.8	13.6	13.0
Federal political	0.0	0.1	0.1	0.1	0.0	0.2	0.1	0.0
Investment credit	0.0	0.3	0.6	0.6	0.0	0.1	0.2	0.7
Dividend tax credit	1.6	31.7	52.8	68.3	1.8	42.3	67.7	81.1
Other credits	95.3	54.8	28.2	8.1	96.2	44.7	18.4	5.2
Total	100.0	100.0	100.0	100.0	100.0	100.0	100.0	100.0

Source: Special tabulations, 1990 Greenbook file (Revenue Canada 1992)

Overall, high-income filers have a greater proportion of investment income and self-employment income. High-income filers show more multiple income sources as income increases. They therefore make correspondingly higher use of the investment-related deductions and tax credits.

High-Income Population over Time

We now examine the characteristics of high-income Ontario filers over time. The database used for this portion of the analysis is the "LAD" – Longitudinal Administrative Database. The LAD is a little-known

Statistics Canada database that merits some general description.[13] It is a 10 per cent random sample of the 1982 Canadian adult population, plus their spouses, constructed from federal tax files. The basic unit of observation is the individual (which is how Canadians file taxes), but records are matched to identify legal and common-law marriages and to add family-level information to each individual's file (total family income, number of children, etc.). The 1982–6 longitudinal element was achieved by matching these individuals' records over time, principally by social insurance number. Thus, Statistics Canada has constructed a very large longitudinal sample containing useful tax-based information on individuals and their families, with the income and tax data – which are key to the present analysis – being of particularly high quality.[14]

In terms of the LAD's sampling properties, upwards of 90 per cent of the adult population is represented in the tax files for the 1982–6 period covered by the data, and the coverage is undoubtedly even better for the high-income population we are interested in here. (Low-income individuals are often not required to file and, before the growth in refundable tax credits, had little incentive to do so.) Checks against the Census and the Survey of Consumer Finances (SCF) in terms of family structure (marital status and number of children), age, income, and other key variables, indicate that the LAD sample is indeed closely representative of the Canadian population.

The specific sample used in the analysis consists of all individuals who had greater than three times median individual income in any one of the five years covered by the LAD.[15] For these purposes, median individual income is taken from the Survey of Consumer Finance and determined with respect to all individuals having positive income in the relevant year (Statistics Canada 1991). The three times median cut-offs for the years 1982–6 were thus (in current dollars): $36,300, $36,600, $37,900, $40,400, and $43,200. Note that high income defined in this way is significantly lower than the definition used in the Greenbook portion of the analysis, partly because the SCF includes non-filing individuals.

Individuals were dropped from the LAD sample if there were any missing records over the five years of data.[16] The sample was further restricted to include only those filers who had ever filed a return in Ontario during one of the five years. The final sample thus consists of the five years of data representing the 72,200 Ontario tax filers who had "high income" in any year 1982–6.[17] As a final verification, the annual data for each of the years in this longitudinal sample were checked against Greenbook figures; the figures line up very closely.

Table 10 first provides a view of high-income dynamics by showing the *number* of years in which those in the sample had high income (remember that *all* individuals who *ever* had high income over the 1982–6 period are included in the data). The figures in the first column of the table indicate that a full 25.8 per cent of the "high-income" individuals met the working definition of high income – three times median income – in only one year out of the five. On the other hand, a third of the sample had high income throughout the entire period. These findings can be compared with the dynamics at the opposite end of the income distribution – those with low incomes – by looking at figures reported by the Economic Council of Canada (1992), which also come from the LAD data. According to these data, in general, there is somewhat more stability at the top of the income spectrum than at the bottom. About one-quarter of the ever-high-income population (25.8 per cent) had high income briefly, while about one-third of the ever-"poor" were in that category briefly. On the other hand, about one-third of those who ever had high income were persistently in that group in all five years, while less than one-quarter of the ever-"poor" had continuously low income for the five-year interval covered by the data.[18] Again, while the stability in incomes is somewhat greater for high- than for low-income filers, the majority (at least two-thirds of high-income filers) fluctuate in and out of high income.

The second column of table 10 presents mean effective tax rates (METRs) by the number of years of high income. The METRs are the average rates over the five-year period covered by the data.[19] Rates rise with the duration of high-income status, as expected (since average five-year income also rises). The third and fourth columns repeat these exercises for *very* high income – defined as *five* times median income – as compared with the three times median used to define "high" income. This group was more volatile, with a considerably higher percentage of those who ever had very high income being at those higher levels for only a year or two, and a smaller percentage having very high income all five years, than was the case for the high-income classification. Again, not surprisingly, METRs rise with the number of years of high income. It is worth noting that only 22.1 per cent of the individuals in the high-income sample *ever* had *very* high income – that is, most of those who *ever* had high income *never* had *very* high income.[20]

The METRs shown are significantly lower than those presented for

TABLE 10

High-Income Dynamics: The Number of Years of High (or Very High) Income for Those Who Ever Had High (or Very High) Income, and Associated METRs, Ontario[a]

Number of years with high (or very high) income	High Income (3 Times Median)		Very High Income (5 Times Median)[b]	
	Per cent of Population	METR of group	Per cent of subsample	METR of group
1 year	25.8	.19	39.9	.20
2 years	14.1	.20	15.7	.23
3 years	12.7	.22	11.2	.25
4 years	13.6	.23	10.6	.26
All 5 years	33.8	.26	22.6	.31
	100.0	.22	100.0	.24
Estimated population	72,200		16,000	

Source: Special tabulations, LAD file

[a] Based on a working sample of the 10 per cent LAD (longitudinal database) of anyone in Ontario having more than three times median income in at least one year 1982–6. The working sample includes an estimated 72,200 individuals. (Population sizes are rounded to the nearest 25 in all the LAD-based tables). See the text for further discussion of the data.

[b] This represents the 22.1 per cent of the "high income" working sample who had "*very* high income" – defined as five times median income – in at least one of the years covered by the data (16,000 individuals). The very-high-income groups represent 8.8, 3.5, 2.5, 2.3, and 5.0 per cent of the full high-income sample across the indicated years.

1990 due largely to averaging. It should, however, be noted that income and payroll taxes have risen since the early and mid-eighties (Grady 1990). There have also been large income tax increases in Ontario – especially for high-income filers – from 1991 to 1993 (Grady 1993), which are not included in this analysis.

Table 11 gives an alternative view of tax rates by showing how high-income tax filers were distributed across different METR ranges (these are the five-year average ETRs, as described above). The first column shows these tax categories for all individuals in the high-income sample; the second column restricts the view to those who had high income *all* five years, and the final set of figures is for those who had *very* high income throughout. The figures show that most individuals in the sample had average tax rates of between .20 and .30, although the more stable high earners tend to be at higher rates – again not surprisingly. Indeed, of the "stable very high" group, a full 62.3 per cent were in the highest tax rate category of .30 to .40. On the other hand, some of the

TABLE 11
Distribution (%) of High-Income Filers across METR Ranges, Ontario

METR range	High-Income Group		
	High (High income at least one year)	Stable high (High income all five years)	Stable very high (Very high income all five years)
.00–.10	5.8	2.6	2.6
.10–.20	21.5	8.5	9.7
.20–.30	65.5	69.7	25.4
.30–.40	7.2	19.2	62.3
>.40	0	0	0
	100.0%	100.0%	100.0%
Estimated population	72,200	24,400	3,600

Source: Special tabulations, LAD file
Note: The first column represents the working sample of high-income filers. The second and third columns represent particular subsamples of the general group. (See notes a and b in table 10.)

exceptions are interesting. For example, 12.3 per cent of those who had very high income in all five years had METRs in the lowest two categories, representing METRs of less than .2. The comparable figure is 11.1 per cent for the stable high group. At the other end, 7.2 per cent of those who had high income only a single year were in the highest METR category.

Table 12 looks at the income–METR relationship a little differently by showing mean METRs by income quintiles (i.e., with the tax filers grouped according to their average incomes over the five years). A progressive tax system would generate higher METRs at higher income levels, and this is indeed generally borne out by the figures. The first column reports METRs for the entire high-income sample, and the rates rise from .17 to .26 from lower- to higher-income quintiles. On the other hand, the rates do not increase substantially; the highest-income earners still had effective tax rates of just over one-quarter. The second and third columns present the results when the sample is restricted to only the stable high- and stable very-high-income individuals, respectively.

Table 13 shows the income–METR relationship in more detail, by showing where the population of high-income tax filers lies on a grid of income and METR quintiles. In general, we would expect those with lower incomes also to have the lowest METRs, those in the middle of

TABLE 12
METRs by Income Quintiles, Ontario[a]

| Income quintile (1990 $) | High-Income Group[b] | | |
	High (high income at least one year)	Stable high (high income all five years)	Stable very high (very high income all five years)
Lowest (<$41,000)	.17	–	–
Second ($41,000–$46,000)	.22	–	–
Third ($46,000–$52,000)	.23	.24	–
Fourth ($52,000–$62,000)	.24	.25	–
Highest ($62,000+)	.26	.27	.31

Source: Special tabulations, LAD file
[a] METRs and income quintiles are based on the high-income sample, and have been computed using averages for the five years covered by the data. Each income quintile consists of approximately 14,450 individuals. All figures are based on at least 2,700 observations.
[b] See note, table 11. The same income quintile groupings are used throughout the table, which is why there are missing cells at the lower quintiles for the more stable groups – that is, there are no "stable high-" income individuals in the bottom quintiles.

the high-income group to be in the middle tax ranges, and those with the highest incomes to have the highest METRs. That is, the sample ought to be heavily concentrated along the diagonal of the table, which has been shaded to facilitate this inspection. Income and METR rankings are, in fact, significantly correlated, as seen in the entries along the diagonal generally being larger than the off-diagonals, and the cells directly adjacent to the diagonal also being quite large. On the other hand, there are some clear outliers. In particular, the figures in the lower-left area of the table indicate that there were significant proportions of the highest income ranges in the lowest effective tax rate groups. These results are consistent with those of the previous tables, but show more clearly how significant numbers of high-income recipients paid relatively low taxes year in and year out.

Table 14 is similar to the previous table, but shows the distribution of the individuals in each five-year income quintile across specified METR *ranges*. The generally progressive nature of the income tax system is again seen: individuals in the higher income quintiles tend to

TABLE 13
Distribution of High-Income Filers (%) by Income and METR Quintiles, Ontario

Income quintile (1990 $)	METR Quintile					
	Lowest (.00–.18)	Second (.18–.20)	Third (.22–.25)	Fourth (.25–.27)	Highest (.27+)	
Lowest (<$41,000)	49.6	29.7	13.8	6.2	0.7	100%
Second ($41,000–$46,000)	13.8	28.3	30.1	22.1	5.7	100%
Third ($46,000–$52,000)	10.4	20.1	28.0	29.9	11.6	100%
Fourth ($52,000–$62,000)	11.0	12.7	19.9	29.8	26.7	100%
Highest ($62,000+)	15.2	9.3	8.3	12.0	55.2	100%
	100.0%	100.0%	100.0%	100.0%	100.0%	

Source: Special tabulations, LAD file
Note: The METR and income quintiles are averages for the five years covered by the data. Each income or METR quintile consists of approximately 14,450 individuals (i.e., row or column).

be in the higher METR brackets. But the significant number of exceptions is perhaps ever better illustrated in this presentation. For example, of those in the highest five-year income quintile, 19.1 per cent had effective tax rates of under .20. Indeed, more of these top-income recipients experienced METRs at this low level than was the case for the third or fourth quintiles, with 16.0 and 15.3 per cent respectively in the lowest two effective tax rate ranges. The 19.1 per cent for the highest income group is in fact just below the 22.8 per cent of the second-lowest group, which has similarly low tax rates.

Conclusions

Individuals with high incomes in Canada and Ontario have gone largely unstudied, while middle- and low-income Canadians receive considerable statistical attention. This study provides a profile of high-income Ontarians focusing on the taxes they paid, and to a lesser extent, on their incomes and demographic composition.

In 1990, 95 per cent of all Ontario tax filers – those receiving less than three times median total income or $65,000 – had average incomes of $23,000; those with incomes above $65,000 averaged $125,000. These so-called high-income filers tend to be middle-aged married men, and more often have multiple sources of income. Because of the general

TABLE 14
Distribution (%) across METR Ranges by Income Quintile, Ontario

Income quintile (1990 $)	METR Range						Mean METR
	.00–.10	.10–.20	.20–.30		.30–.40		
Lowest (<$41,000)	14.6	48.9	⟶	36.6	⟵	100.0%	.17
Second ($41,000–$46,000)	3.1	19.7	⟶	77.2	⟵	100.0%	.22
Third ($46,000–$52,000)	2.9	13.1	83.7		0.3	100.0%	.23
Fourth ($52,000–$62,000)	3.4	11.9	81.6		3.1	100.0%	.24
Highest ($62,000+)	5.0	14.1	48.5		32.4	100.0%	.26

Source: Special tabulations, LAD file
⟵⟶ Cells merged due to sample size less than 25.
Note: The METRs and income quintiles are averages for the five years covered by the data. Each income quintile consists of approximately 14,450 individuals.

progressivity of the personal income tax system, high-income filers experience average effective tax rates more than double those of non–high-income filers. However, the top income percentile group has a greater proportion of filers with effective tax rates of 10 per cent or lower than do all income decile groups above the median. The greater reliance on investment income, combined with a more favourable treatment of that income compared with labour income in the tax system, give rise to these results.

There is considerable volatility of high incomes, with most individuals who had ever had "high incomes" in any year from 1982 to 1986 moving in and out of "high income." On the other hand, there also appears to be more stability among high-income individuals than among those at the bottom end of the income distribution. The general relationships between income and taxes, including the existence of high income–low tax rate individuals, are stable over time.

Notes

The authors gratefully acknowledge the very capable research assistance of Ernest Rix and Susan Carruthers. The authors accept full responsibility for any errors or omissions and for all views expressed herein. The analysis should not be taken as representing the views of Statistics Canada.

1 See Wolfson and Evans 1990 for a description of a number of Canadian low-income lines.

2 In this and all subsequent tables, no data for fewer than 25 individuals is displayed. All percentiles have been rounded to the nearest $100 and all incomes used in the calculation of average income figures to the nearest $1000.

3 Most readers will likely be accustomed to income data presented for families. While family income is important in determining who are the "rich," it is outside the scope of this study, largely because of data deficiencies. The data sources with the most complete and reliable data on high-income Ontarians (i.e., the Greenbook) have no family information. On the other hand, recent survey data that include good family income information, such as the Survey of Consumer Finances, lack a sufficient sample of high-income individuals.

4 The average loss in the bottom five percentile group is due to the averaging of large losses in the first percentile with small incomes in the next four percentiles.

5 Where median family income was adjusted for equivalent adult units.

6 1988 Canadian dollars adjusted for international comparisons using purchasing power parities.

7 We assume for this calculation that only the basic personal credit is claimed. Persons with total incomes higher than $70,000 may not, in fact, have to pay any surtax – i.e., because of additional dependents or use of tax expenditures. The key point is that no one with total income less than $70,000 will ever have to pay the surtax.

8 The Revenue Canada Taxation Statistics (1992) publication presents taxable capital gains and taxable dividend income. These components of income have been adjusted to represent total income from these sources (i.e., dividend income is divided by 5/4 and capital gains is divided by 3/4).

9 They are slightly lower than maximum combined federal plus provincial statutory rates in the tax system because they have been averaged across filers with different levels of income and deductions. The jump in marginal tax rates for investment income in 1988 was due to the elimination of the $1,000 interest deduction.

10 This variability points to the fact that the highest-income groups having the highest ETRs (top 1 or top 0.1) vary as a percentage of the top 5 group. That is, the upper tail (skewness) of the distribution varies by occupation.

11 The counts are rounded to the nearest 25.

12 Note that dividends are treated in a special two-step manner for tax pur-

poses. First they are "grossed up" by 25 per cent to reflect the *assumed* underlying corporate profits tax paid by firms before their profits are distributed to shareholders. Then these grossed-up dividends are eligible for a non-refundable tax credit intended to compensate for the corporate-level profits taxes already assumed to be paid. This complex treatment of dividend income derives from proposals for corporate and personal tax integration made by the Carter Royal Commission in 1966. However, the currently implemented version takes no account of corporate-level tax expenditures, and thus often assumes full statutory taxes were paid when in fact the underlying corporate profits were taxed at much lower effective rates. Unfortunately, no data are available to analyse effective tax rates on a truly integrated basis.

13 The construction of the LAD database was a joint undertaking of Statistics Canada and the former Economic Council of Canada.

14 For a more detailed discussion of the LAD database, see Finnie 1993.

15 Because the LAD constitutes a 10 per cent sample of tax filers *plus* their spouses, there is an overrepresentation of married individuals in the sample. That is, while unmarried individuals are included at the 10 per cent rate, some married individuals are in the LAD due to their being married to other individuals in the 10 per cent sample, and not just being in the 10 per cent sample themselves. On the other hand, the procedures used below to select high-income individuals result in such "extra spouses," who did not themselves have high incomes in any year, being dropped from the working sample. Checks indicate that the remaining overrepresentation of married individuals in the high-income sample is quite small.

16 Records are missing when the individual did not file a tax form. Reasons for not filing include: being absent from the country, having low enough income that filing was not required, late filing, and death. Records are also missing if the individual's records were not matched across years; a full longitudinal file could not be constructed in such cases. Overall, 90 per cent of Ontario tax filers who had three times median income in any year 1982–6 had records for all five years.

17 All sample sizes are rounded to the nearest 25, while income figures are rounded to the nearest $1,000.

18 It was noted earlier that the LAD data used in the poverty analysis carried out by the Economic Council probably underrepresent low-income individuals. Their results should be seen in this context, although some ancillary analysis by the Council researchers suggested that their major findings would not be significantly changed by the inclusion of the missing individuals. Further, while certain income sources that are important

to low-income Canadians are excluded from the LAD – social assistance in particular – these income sources tend to have little effect on poverty status per se (i.e., they are generally insufficient to bring individuals over the poverty threshold). In any event, the Economic Council figures are the only ones that exist for Canada, and provide a useful broad reference for the high-income dynamics revealed in the present study.

19 That is, we first calculate the ETR for each individual for each year (defined as in the previous section as total federal plus provincial income plus payroll taxes divided by total income. Income is net of business expenses, but not standard individual or personal deductions. CPP/QPP deductions and UI premiums are included as taxes). We then calculate the average ETR for each individual for the five years covered by the data. Finally, the table shows the means of these five-year average rates across individuals with the indicated characteristics.

20 Only 5.0 per cent of the individuals in the entire high-income sample have *very* high income in all five years.

Bibliography

Bordt, M., G. Cameron, S. Gribble, B. Murphy, G. Rowe, and M. Wolfson. 1990. "The Social Policy Simulation Database and Model." *Canadian Tax Journal* 38(1) (January): 48–65

Buhman, B., L. Rainwater, G. Schmaus, and T. Smeeding. 1988. "Equivalence Scales, Well-Being, Inequality, and Poverty: Sensitivity Estimates across Ten Countries Using the Luxembourg Income Study Database." *The Review of Income and Wealth* 34 (June)

Danzinger S., P. Gottschalk, and E. Smolensky. 1989. "How the Rich Have Fared, 1973–87." *AEA Papers and Proceedings* 79(2) (May): 310–14

Economic Council of Canada. 1992. "The New Face of Poverty: Income Security Needs of Canadian Families." Ottawa: Economic Council of Canada

Fair Tax Commission. 1993. *Searching for Fairness*. Discussion Paper. Toronto

Finnie, Ross. 1993. "Women, Men, and the Economic Consequences of Divorce: Evidence from Canadian Longitudinal Data." *Canadian Review of Sociology and Anthropology* 30(2) (May): 205–41

Grady, P. 1990. "The Distributional Impact of the Federal Tax and Transfer Changes Introduced Since 1984." *Canadian Tax Journal* 38(2) (March): 286–97

– 1993. "Ontario NDP Tax Increases." *Canadian Business Economics* 1(4) (Summer): 12–23

OECD. 1982. *The OECD List of Social Indicators*. Paris: OECD

Pen, Jan. 1971. *Income Distribution*. New York: Praeger

Revenue Canada Taxation. 1992. *1990 Taxation Statistics* (the "Greenbook").
Ottawa: Revenue Canada

Ruggles, P. 1990. *Drawing the Line: Alternative Poverty Measures and Their
Implications for Public Policy*. Washington, DC: The Urban Institute Press

Statistics Canada. 1991. *Income Distributions by Size in Canada 1990*. Statistics
Canada Catalogue 13–207. Ottawa.

U.S. Bureau of the Census. 1987. *A Marketer's Guide to Discretionary Income*.
Washington, DC

Wolfson, Michael. 1989. "Inequality and Polarization: Is There a Disappearing Middle Class?" In Proceedings of the Statistics Canada Symposium on
Analysis of Data in Time. October 1989. Ottawa: Statistics Canada

– 1993. "When Inequalities Diverge." A paper presented to the American
Economics Association. January 1994. Boston

Wolfson, Michael, and John Evans. 1990. *Statistics Canada's Low Income Cut-
Offs: Methodological Concerns and Possibilities*. Ottawa: Statistics Canada

Wolfson, M.C., and B.B. Murphy. 1992. "Kinder and Gentler – A Compara-
tive Analysis of Incomes of the Elderly in Canada and the U.S." A paper
prepared for the Meeting of the North American Economics and Finance
Association. New Orleans

Notes on Contributors

Ross Finnie is Assistant Professor of Economics, Laval University. He is currently visiting at Statistics Canada.

Brian Murphy is a senior researcher in the Analytical Studies Branch of Statistics Canada.

Sheila M. Block is Assistant Director of Research of the Fair Tax Commission.

Richard Shillington has graduate degrees in statistics from the University of Waterloo. He is the principal of an Ottawa-based consulting firm specializing in quantitative research on socioeconomic policy. He has conducted research on health and socioeconomic policies for various levels of government.

Michael Wolfson is Director General of the Analytical Studies Branch, Statistics Canada.

Ken Battle is President of the Caledon Institute of Social Policy, a non-profit organization for social policy research and development and public education.

Sherri Torjman is Research Associate at the Caledon Institute of Social Policy and an independent consultant on social policy.

Commission Organization

Chair**
Monica Townson

Vice-Chairs
Neil Brooks*
Robert Couzin*

Commissioners
Jayne Berman
William Blundell
Susan Giampietri
Brigitte Kitchen*
Gérard Lafrenière
Fiona Nelson
Satya Poddar*

Executive Director
Hugh Mackenzie

Director of Research
Allan M. Maslove

Assistant Director of Research
Sheila Block

Executive Assistant to Research Program
Moira Hutchinson

Editorial Assistant
Marguerite Martindale

*Member of the Research Subcommittee
**Chair of the Research Subcommittee

www.ingramcontent.com/pod-product-compliance
Lightning Source LLC
Chambersburg PA
CBHW030524210326
41597CB00013B/1022